NEURO-PHILOSOPHY
AND THE HEALTHY MIND

NEURO-PHILOSOPHY
AND THE **HEALTHY MIND**

Learning from the Unwell Brain

GEORG NORTHOFF

W.W. Norton & Company

NEW YORK / LONDON

For information about permission to reproduce selections
from this book, write to Permissions, W. W. Norton & Company, Inc., 500 Fifth Avenue, New York, NY 10110

For information about special discounts for bulk purchases,
please contact W. W. Norton Special Sales at specialsales@
wwnorton.com or 800-233-4830

Manufacturing by Maple Press
Book design by Carole Desnoes
Production manager: Christine Critelli

Library of Congress Cataloging-in-Publication Data

Northoff, Georg, author.
Neuro-philosophy and the healthy mind : learning from the
unwell brain
/ Georg Northoff. — First edition.
p. ; cm.
Includes bibliographical references and index.
ISBN 978-0-393-70938-4 (pbk.)
I. Title.
[DNLM: 1. Brain—physiology. 2. Consciousness—physiology.
3. Philosophy, Medical. WL 300]
QP376
611'.81—dc23

2015024278

W. W. Norton & Company, Inc.
500 Fifth Avenue, New York, N.Y. 10110
www.wwnorton.com

W. W. Norton & Company Ltd.
Castle House, 75/76 Wells Street, London W1T 3QT

1 2 3 4 5 6 7 8 9 0

I dedicate this book to all of my patients, students, and collaborators, who have provided me with much insight.

CONTENTS

PREFACE AND ACKNOWLEDGMENTS

Neuroscience is a young kid. Given the research boom these days, one cannot imagine that neuroscience, as a field of study, is only 100–150 years old. At the turn of the 19th to the 20th century there were no imaging/scanning devices available that could provide direct and online insight into the functioning of the brain. One source of information, however, was the clinical cases reported in neurology and psychiatry journals. The brains of patients with abnormal mental features could provide some clues about brain functioning, especially via postmortem investigation of structural abnormalities such as lesions. Despite the fact that we have fancy tools such as fMRI (functional magnetic resonance imaging) equipment these days, we nevertheless have not yet unravelled the puzzle of how the dull gray matter of the brain can generate something as colourful as the various mental features we think of as *self*, *consciousness*, *emotional feelings*, and *personal identity*.

Returning to the origins of neuroscience to study the unwell brain for clues about the healthy mind brings me to the added element in the title of my book, *Neuro-Philosophy and the Healthy Mind: Learning from the Unwell Brain*:

philosophy. Over the centuries it has been philosophers who discussed and described mental features and their concepts. These particular concepts often have been carried over into the context of neuroscience, without thorough investigation of whether such one-to-one transfer from mind to brain is really feasible and plausible. By comparing and correlating neuroscientific data and philosophical definitions of various mental concepts—for example, self, consciousness, emotional feelings, and personal identity—I reveal some major discrepancies between neuroscience and philosophy that we can overcome and bridge only by changing how we define our mental concepts in philosophy. Hence, *Neuro-Philosophy and the Healthy Mind: Learning from the Unwell Brain* carries major implications not only for how researchers in neuroscience and clinicians understand and view the brain in relation to psychiatric disorders, but also for the various kinds of puzzles often discussed by past and present philosophers.

I want to thank Deborah Malmud and Benjamin Yarling from W.W. Norton & Company for their excellent support in the different stages of producing the book. Benjamin Yarling was particularly helpful in giving excellent feedback and recommendations about style and structure in the writing of a transdisciplinary book at the intersecting edges of neuroscience, psychiatry, and philosophy. Mark Burgess earns my thanks for his helpful editing of earlier versions of the book, and Nils Frederic Wagner and Annemarie Wolf for reading some of the final chapters. I also thank Wendy Carter for organizing the references, and the director of our institute, the University of Ottawa Institute of Mental Health Research (IMHR), Dr. Zul Merali, for giving me the free mental (and also physical) space to develop and articulate my ideas and views of the brain, including how it is related to the mind and its mental features. Finally, I want to thank John Sarkissian for his patience and support during the long hours, days, and sometimes weeks of mental (as well as physical) absence.

NEURO-PHILOSOPHY
AND THE **HEALTHY MIND**

INTRODUCTION

How does the mind relate to the brain? This is *the* big question of our time. Much has been resolved in terms of the role of evolution, the unconscious, and most recently, the genetic contribution. The nature of the mind and its origin in the brain, though, has remained elusive so far. How can we gain a better understanding of what the mind is? In fact, what is it that we think of when we talk about the mind? Let's consider the following imaginary case scenario:

You are having tea with your friend, who is about 34 years old and an established journalist. You are talking about the bad weather, how cold it is, and discuss the latest fashion in winter coats that promises full protection against the daunting wind. Your friend vividly describes the beautiful coat she recently bought, then suddenly stops talking. After a few moments she starts stuttering only one term, "kon," which she repeats slowly several times. You ask her "What's wrong?" She does not answer. You ask again. No response. The only answer you get is "kon." Now you realize that something must be seriously wrong. You call 9-1-1 and the ambulance comes.

This is the situation Paul Broca (1824–1880), a famous French neurologist and anthropologist, faced in the middle of the 19th century. He encountered several patients who, all of a sudden, were unable to articulate and express themselves through speech or language and stopped talking altogether for the rest of their lives. However, these patients still appeared to comprehend what was said to them. His first and most famous patient got the nickname "Tan" because he could only pronounce one word, "tan." Most interestingly, investigating this man's brain after his death, Broca observed that he had suffered from a lesion in a specific part of the brain, the left frontal lobe, which lies in the anterior part beneath the forehead. Because Broca confirmed this correlation between the symptom and the brain location by observing the same lesion in the brains of other deceased patients' who had suffered from similar speech deficits (called now *expressive* or *motor aphasia*), this region in the brain has since been named "Broca's area."

Following Broca, Carl Wernicke (1848–1905), a German doctor, observed some patients who exhibited a slightly different pattern of deficits. These patients were unable to understand speech, but they could produce words and speech. They could still speak and articulate words, so their repertoire was not limited to one particular word like "kin" or "tan." However, their speech and the way in which they combined words made no sense anymore; it was meaningless "word salad," as this kind of speech came to be described.

Your friend would not have stopped talking altogether, but rather would have suddenly started to mix words up so that you would not have understood anything. Despite the fact that she would have been able to pronounce words correctly, the combination of these words would have amounted to gibberish. The primary deficit here is not in the expression or motor articulation of speech, but in its reception or sensory processing. This type of aphasia is therefore called *receptive* or *sensory aphasia* (instead of expressive or motor aphasia). Rather than being associated with the frontal cortex, as is Broca's region, Wernicke found the main lesion in these patients to be more posterior in the brain, in the superior temporal cortex, now called Wernicke's area.

What do these examples from the historical origins of neuroscience in the 19th century tell us? Deficits in speech and their underlying lesions in the brain revealed that higher-order cognitive functions such as language, which characterize humans, are related to the brain. Specifically, these cases show that language is not a homogeneous entity but can be broken down into different domains, such as articulating–motor and receptive–sensory, which are related to different regions in the brain (Broca's and Wernicke's areas, respectively). Since then, research has shown that language is a highly complex function involving several processes and a wide variety of different regions in the brain.

Most importantly, these cases demonstrate that we can learn something about the brain and how it functions from our patients and their symptoms. Such a perspective worked well in the case of language. Why not try the same approach for understanding the mind and investigate abnormalities in mental features such as self, consciousness, emotional feelings, and personal identity? Such an approach leads us to neurological patients in vegetative states and to psychiatric patients suffering from depression or schizophrenia. My overarching aim in this book is to demonstrate what we can learn from these patients and their unwell brains to increase our understanding of how the healthy mind works. As with other situations in life, sometimes it is the malfunctions that help us understand how things work.

The "Hard Problem" of the Mind

The human mind has various unique features: There is consciousness, our sense of self, something that accounts for our personal identity over time, emotions, cognition, free will, among others. The most central and basic of all these mental features is consciousness. Without consciousness, nothing else matters—or so it seems. But what is consciousness? For most of our lives, we are conscious if we are awake (i.e., not asleep). There are, of course, exceptions such as situations when we undergo surgery and are being anesthetized, or when we have a motorcyle accident resulting in the loss of consciousness.

Consciousness is one of the biggest puzzles still confronting researchers and thinkers in many fields. Why and how can something as subjective and colorful as personal experience—that is, consciousness—arise from our brains—something that is objective and a rather dull gray in color? This is what the contemporary Australian philosopher David Chalmers (1996) called the "hard problem," and it is indeed a tough nut to crack. All the fancy tools of neuroscience that are used these days to investigate the brain show us different neuronal features of brain functioning. These neuronal mechanisms—the inner workings and elaborations of the brain—are better and better understood. However, none of these tools show us why and how the neuronal features of the brain are transformed into the mental features of consciousness, self, or emotional feelings. Despite all the progress, something very crucial is nevertheless lacking in current neuroscience and its account of the brain—the answer to the hard problem is still missing.

What precisely is lacking in current neuroscience and its view of the brain? Our brain processes the various contents or inputs it receives from its own body and the environment. That is the easy part of the puzzle and remains beyond dispute. However, additionally, the brain seems to add an extra factor that transforms the *purely objective processing of contents into subjective experience*. We do not just process the color red in an objective way; we experience the redness of, say, a ripe tomato in a very subjective way. This is what the philosopher Thomas Nagel (1974) described as the "what it is like" part of our experiences that characterizes our consciousness as intrinsically subjective rather than as merely objective.

Where does this "what it is like" feature of consciousness come from? Past philosophers such as René Descartes assumed from some kind of immaterial soul that exists within the body and brain. This soul was supposed to account for the subjective nature of human experience and hence for mental features like consciousness and self. Nowadays such an assumption of an immaterial soul separate from brain and body is largely obsolete. How, though, can we then explain the "what it is like," the subjective nature of mental features, if there is nothing but a seemingly objective brain? This question leads us straight back to the "hard problem": Why and how is there consciousness rather than nonconsciousness and mere brain material?

Does the brain itself add this subjective component, the "what it is like" aspect? All kinds of objective neuronal mechanisms have been suggested in current neuroscience and philosophy fields in order to account for the subjectivity of human experience. We will discuss some of these mechanisms in the course of this book. But, as we will see, none of them can explain why and how the objective neuronal states of the brain are transformed into the subjective mental features of consciousness. Why and how are the neuronal features of the brain transformed into mental features? This is the question guiding our investigations into the brain. In our search for answers to this question, we will go deeply into both philosophy and neuroscience, or *neurophilosophy*, as it is called these days.

Neurophilosophy

What is neurophilosophy? Neuroscientists increasingly venture into the originally philosophical territory of the mind and its mental features. There they are confronted with mental concepts of consciousness, self, emotions, identity, free will, and many others. These concepts were originally defined in the context of philosophy, with its spiritually oriented baggage, and therefore the baggage resurfaces with the concepts in neuroscience. How shall we deal with the philosophical baggage in the concepts we use to describe mental features?

The opinions differ widely. Some traditionally minded philosophers such as Thomas Nagel, Peter Hacker, and Colin McGinn argue that mental concepts cannot be researched empirically at all; the question of the mind, whether seen as materially caused or not, escapes scientific methods and thus remains a philosophical one that cannot be addressed in neuroscience. These proponents state that the mind exclusively belongs to philosophy, and hence has no place in neuroscience. In a nutshell, neuroscience is, and can only be, about the brain, whereas philosophy addresses the mind.

However, the opposite extreme is much more popular and can be found in what is described these days as neurophilosophy. Having developed predominantly in the Anglo-American world, neurophilosophers such as Patricia and Paul Churchland and John Bickle argue that there is no need any more for any kind of mental concepts. Put in rather broad and general terms, one may summarize their convictions in the following way: "Throw overboard the mental concepts such as self, free will, and consciousness and replace them with the neural concepts of the brain," we hear them shouting. "There is no mind; there is only the brain" is their claim. However, despite all the progress in neuroscience, even these emphatic neurophilosophers did not provide convincing answers to the question of how the brain transforms neuronal activity into mental features.

Most neurophilosophers currently argue that the mind is the brain and that its various mental features are nothing but manifestations of the neural features of the brain. They provide various arguments and theories that, despite being elegant in their logical analysis, ultimately fail to provide an answer to the question of neuronal–mental transformations. Why do they fail? They leave open the exact mechanisms by means of which the brain and its not yet fully clear neural features are transformed into mental features and thus generate consciousness.

How can we investigate the turning point, the moment, in which the brain's neural activity is transformed into mental features? When, for instance, is a particular neural state of the brain associated with a mental state such as consciousness and when is it not? We currently do not know. Neuroscience increasingly understands how the brain works, operates, and functions. However, neuroscience has not yet fully elucidated why the very same neuronal features lead to mental features as they are described in philosophy.

From Unwell Brains to Healthy Minds

How can we change our philosophical preconception such that we can get a grip on how the brain transforms its neuronal activity into mental features? Neuroscience usually investigates the healthy brain. Philosophy focuses on the healthy mind. Both seek to explain how mental features such as self and consciousness come into being. What philosophers have discussed in previous centuries regarding the mind is now put into the context of the brain. For instance, Descartes's assumption of the soul as a special faculty underlying mental features now resurfaces as a specific region, network, or mechanism within the brain. The term *mental* is often simply replaced by the term *neuronal*. Mental features are declared to be neuronal features. That shift, though, still leaves unexplained how the seemingly objective neuronal features of the brain can generate something as subjective as mental features. In short, the question of neuronal–mental transformation remains open.

Though desirable in a broad sense, the collaboration between philosophy and neuroscience seems to have transferred the "old" problem of the mind–brain relationship into the "new" context of the brain. The traditional dualism imposed between mind and brain resurfaces within the dualism between two kinds of neuronal features: those that are purely neuronal and those that are relevant to mental features. The brain–brain problem replaces the mind–brain problem. There is thus a deadlock between philosophy and neuroscience: The originally metaphysical concepts and ideas of the former are reinforced and implemented within the empirical context of the brain.

How can we escape this deadlock between philosophy and neuroscience? We need another source outside both fields and their mental and neuronal concepts. One such possible source is neurological and psychiatric disorders. The loss of consciousness due to brain injury that produces a vegetative state may tell us something important about how the healthy brain transforms its neuronal features into states of consciousness. Similarly, the alterations in self, emotional feeling, and personal identity that characterize psychiatric disorders such as depression or schizophrenia will help to reveal some previously unclear secrets about the healthy mind and how it is related to the brain.

Broca and Wernicke learned about language and how it is related to the brain from their patients. Analogously, I take neurological and psychiatric disorders involving abnormalities in self, consciousness, emotional feelings, and personal identity as the starting point for investigating the yet unclear relationship between neuronal functions and mental features. These disorders reveal how the workings of unwell brains differ from the healthy brain. Most importantly, the unwell brains tell us, in an indirect way, about the mechanisms that transform neuronal functions into mental features in a healthy mind (Searle, 2004).

Bottom line: My aim is to infer the healthy *mind* from the unwell *brain*. This will also tell us whether, and if so, how, we must change our philosophical concepts in order to properly describe what philosophers call *mind* and *brain*.

I invite you to join me on a journey that takes us from case examples of fictive patients with neurological or psychiatric disorders, inspired by my clinical experience as a psychiatrist, to fascinating neuroimaging investigations that I am working on as a neuroscientist. Last but not least, we will consider new, wide-ranging theories of mind and brain that I encounter in my work as a neurophilosopher.

Chapter 1

LOSS OF CONSCIOUSNESS

 PREVIEW

How can we search for the brain behind the mind?

What is the mind? Philosophers have long speculated about the nature of the mind and its various mental states. Consciousness is seen as the main feature of the mind, but this view entails a pressing question: How is consciousness related to the body and its brain? Recent research in neuroscience suggests that mental features such as consciousness are based in the brain and its neural activity. Why and how, though, is the neural activity of the brain transformed into the mental features that we associate with consciousness? We currently do not know. I suggest learning from the opposite: from the *loss* of consciousness. The neural changes involved in the loss of consciousness should give us indirect clues about the neural mechanisms underlying its presence. I begin this chapter with an imaginary though typical case example of a patient experiencing a loss of consciousness; that experience, in turn, serves as blueprint for raising questions about the brain and its neuronal–mental features.

CASE EXAMPLE

When John was 5 years old, his neighbor had a boyfriend who rode a BMW motorcycle, a powerful black machine that she would gleefully hop onto and then disappear in a blur down the otherwise quiet street. John used to sit out in front of his house and await their return. His favorite part was watching his neighbor hop off the bike, release her curly red hair from the helmet, kiss her boyfriend goodbye, and bound up the steps to her house.

Now 21 years old, he was thinking of this neighbor and the boyfriend (whose name he never even knew but who had become a kind of vague ideal, a distant pillar of his emerging sense of self) as he rode his own new BMW bike over to his girlfriend Lucie's apartment. They had been together for half a year and had been certain, for most of that time, that they were in love. He had been imagining this day, in some ways, since before they had even met.

It could hardly have been a more perfect day. Most of their college friends had left town for Thanksgiving week-end, leaving John and Lucie feeling like happy fugitives as they reached the city's outskirts and found the two-lane highway, climbing up into the hills decorated with red- and yellow-colored trees as the warm wind blew past their smil-ing faces. The ride felt just as John had imagined it would. They turned off the highway onto a narrow road without any traffic, leaving them more time to embrace the distractions. Lucie wrapped her arms a little tighter around John's waist and rested her head on his back, closing her eyes. John was thinking of the picnic spot he had been planning for weeks, with the willow tree hanging over the creek, when a pickup truck sprang up one of the hills without warning. John saw it immediately, but in his reveries he had drifted to the middle of the narrow road, and the only thing he could do was to violently thrust the handlebars in the direction of the ditch. The road went quiet except for the scraping of something on gravel. The autumn trees spun and then went dark. John and Lucie lost consciousness.

The truck stopped and the driver found two people lying on the street, unresponsive except for the unmistakable rise and fall of their chests—they were still breathing. The driver called the ambulance. It arrived within 10 minutes and both John and Lucie were taken to the hospital and put on life support. Neither of them was reacting in any way; only some small eye movements could be observed, especially in Lucie. The doctors diagnosed John with an unresponsive wakefulness state/vegetative state (UWS/VS), and Lucie with a minimally conscious state (MCS). For the first week after the accident they remained in the intensive care unit without showing any improvement in their level of consciousness. They were then moved to the normal unit, where they stayed for the next 4 weeks, but since their level of consciousness did not improve, they were transferred to a rehabilitation hospital.

From Neural Disorder to Mental Order

Now you probably want to know about the outcome of Lucie and John. Did they ever wake up again? Or will they stay in this condition until the end of their lives? We will come back to them and their fate. First, though, we need to consider some basic issues in a new way. What exactly happened here? John and Lucie lost their consciousness. What is consciousness? Tentatively put, when we are conscious, we are awake and able to respond to the environment. In contrast, we are no longer awake or responding to events in the environment during a dreamless sleep (in this definition, dreams are a form of consciousness as well). How about Lucie and John? John's level of consciousness is very low; he does not respond, does not seem to experience anything at all, does not show even minimal or micro movements. His general condition, as just noted, is called *unresponsive wakefulness/vegetative state* (UWS/VS). John's eyes are still open; if they are closed completely and no reaction at all can be elicited, one speaks of coma.

In contrast, there is a minimal sense of consciousness preserved in Lucie, who may respond, to a minimal degree, with minimal signs of motor behavior. Her condition is consequently called *minimally conscious state* (MCS). UWS/VS and MCS often occur after motorcycle accidents (especially involving young men) or other similar types of trauma whereby the brain is severely damaged. Take the case of the famous Formula One driver, Michael Schumacher, who lost consciousness after a ski accident and was in a VS. It can also happen to older people with lesions in their brain following a stroke, bleeding, or tumor. The brain appears to shut down, closing the door to consciousness. That's what happened to Ariel Sharon, the former Israeli prime minister, who was in a coma for about 5 years before he finally died.

How can we help these patients recover their level of consciousness? We currently do not have any therapeutic means available, nor do we understand why and how they lose their consciousness. You may also ask what exactly *consciousness* refers to and how we can define it. In the case of John and Lucie, their level of arousal is simply too low to assign consciousness to specific contents. They consequently seem to remain unable to experience contents, such as the sounds coming from the hospital corridors or the voices of people talking to them, in a conscious way. This is clinically manifested in the absence of any movements and motor reaction to stimuli from the outside world.

Consciousness is about contents: the perception and naming of people, events, and conditions around us. Additionally, we are usually also conscious about ourselves. When I look into the mirror in the morning, I become aware of myself; that is, I recognize that this is the same person as yesterday. That is called *self*. This sense of self, or *self-consciousness*, presents neuroscientists with one of their greatest challenges. All they can observe is the brain and its neural activity. There is nothing like a self structure in the brain. Despite the apparent absence of self in the neural activity of the brain, we nevertheless have the continuous experience of a self. In short, the self seems to be neurally absent but experientially present. How about Lucie and John? Does the loss of consciousness entail their loss of a sense of self too? Or, alternatively, does their sense of self persist even during the loss of consciousness? We currently do not know.

In addition to urgent clinical questions underlying the condition of these patients are more fundamental questions about how our brains yield mental features that coalesce into consciousness and a sense of self. The sense of self is especially altered in psychiatric disorders such as depression and schizophrenia, as noted previously. Patients with depression experience their sense of self only in an extremely negative way, associated with guilt, shame, and failure, and some patients with schizophrenia actually experience a different self when, for instance, they claim to be

Jesus or some other famous personality. What happens to the brain in these cases?

Disorders like vegetative states, depression, and schizophrenia lead us to even more fundamental questions about something philosophers have discussed for about 2,000 years: the nature of the mind. Disorders of the brain can reveal the mechanisms underlying the order of mind. The exploration of neural disorder leads us into the rather shadowy territory between the clinic, neuroscience, and philosophy. Though not fully clear at this point in time, this territory— the realm of brain disorders—may reveal some clues about mental order: about why and how the neural states of the brain are transformed into mental states such as consciousness.

Is the Mind in the Brain?

From early in human history, the mind has been seen as related to specific organs in the body such as the heart and brain. The ancient Egyptians, for example, as far back as the third millennium B.C.E., thought the heart was the locus of the mind even though old scripts show that they were aware of the brain's existence. Later, in ancient Greece, the medical doctor and philosopher Hippocrates hinted at the significance of the brain:

> Men ought to know that from the brain and the brain only arise our pleasures, joys, laughter, and jests as well as sorrows, pain, grief, and tears. . . . It is the same thing which makes us mad or delirious. Inspires us with dread and fear, whether by night or by day, brings us sleeplessness, inopportune mistakes, aimless anxieties, absent

mindedness, and acts that are contrary to habit (Hippocrates, 2006; Jones, 1868).

Despite Hippocrates's emphasis on the brain, other ancient
Greek philosophers, including Plato and Aristotle, preferred
to associate mental features with a mind or soul. Throughout the Middle Ages and even into 16th-century Europe, the
mind became associated with a specific mental substance.
This mental substance, the French philosopher René Descartes (1596–1650) believed, must be distinguished from
the body as physical substance. The brain, though, has two
hemispheres. Descartes knew that already. Does this mean
that we have two minds? No, that is not possible either.
Descartes consequently looked for those parts of the brain
that existed only once, rather than doubled in right and left
hemispheres. He found such a structure in a little endocrine
gland, the pineal gland, which is situated the very middle of
the brain. He thought that the mind and body were somehow connected in this pineal gland (Descartes, Weissman,
& Bluhm, 1996).

Descartes can be considered the father of the modern
question about the relationship between mind and brain:
how, for instance, can the mind be defined, and how does its
existence and reality relate to that of the physical world of
body and brain? This issue is called the *mind–body problem* or the *mind–brain problem*, a term that describes the
relationship between the existence and reality of the mind
and brain.

This conundrum has led to intense discussion among
philosophers and scientists ever since. Some have even
attempted to prove the existence of a mind experimentally.
For example, at the beginning of the 20th century, the phy-

sician Duncan MacDougall (1907) of Boston—in an attempt to provide evidence for the existence of a mind or soul in the form of a mental substance—weighed his patients shortly before and immediately after death. He assumed that the mind or soul leaves the body after death and that, as a mental substance, the mind should have some kind of weight. This led him to suggest that the body would be lighter after death, upon the soul's departure from the body.

Indeed, Dr. MacDougall observed that two of his patients were lighter after death, a difference in weight he attributed to the departure of the mind or soul and its mental substance. In contrast, he did not observe this change in weight in dogs, which were assumed to not have souls. These results were proof enough for him that the mind or soul is a mental substance distinct from the body. Based on his experiment, MacDougall decided that the mind weighed 21 grams.

We now take such determination of the mind in terms of physical weight to be absurd. But are we so different in our current determinations of the mind? The investigation of the mind's physical weight has been replaced by the search for regions or networks in the brain that are specifically related to consciousness and other mental features. For instance, a set of regions in the middle of the brain, the so-called *cortical midline structures*, is often associated with internal thoughts related to the self. In contrast, sensory regions such as the visual or auditory cortex are associated with the processing of external stimuli from the environment. Hence, the localization resurfaces even in our current understanding of the brain when we localize mental features like internal thoughts or sensory features.

What McDougall weighted as mind at his time resurfaces in the brain scans of our time that show colourful dots and spots in specific regions or networks during, for instance, random thoughts and introspection. Do those dots and spots determine the mind? Neuroscientists say yes. Philosophers say no. So what, then, is the mind? Traditionally, features such as consciousness, sense of self, emotional feeling, identity, and free will are considered mental and are attributed to the mind. Analogously, you attribute your right hand and your left leg to the physical features of the body. Let us therefore define the mind in terms of its manifestations and parts, the various mental features.

What are these mental features? That may raise yet another problem. The fact that we have to ask this question means that there is a presumed dualism between mind and brain: They must be characterized by different kinds of existence and reality, namely mental (mind) reality and physical (brain) reality. This position can be traced back to Descartes, and is still advocated by many philosophers today, for example, by Colin McGinn (1991), who, in a nutshell, argues for dualism between mental and physical properties. Discussing various options and versions of dualism is the main focus of what is now called *philosophy of mind*. This term refers to the discussion of the metaphysical existence and reality of the mind and mental features such as consciousness, free will, and the self.

Philosophy of mind is now often considered the primary and most basic among the various philosophical branches. The well-known contemporary philosopher John R. Searle (2004) called it "first philosophy," meaning that the question of the mind is not only the most important one but also provides the foundation for most other philosophical questions—for instance, metaphysical ones about existence and epistemological ones about knowledge. The mind is the real puzzle of our times. Do we have a mind? Or is that what philosophers call *mind* nothing but the physical structure of the brain? It's a problem philosophers have struggled with for centuries, but we won't join them in those struggles here. Instead we'll focus on the brain itself and what it's doing during the state many of us love most: the resting state.

How can we bridge the gap between brain and mind, between neuronal and mental features? Throughout this book I show that the resting state of the brain and its particular spatial–temporal configuration provide the necessary input to bridge the gap between what we observe as neuronal activity and what we experience as mental features. This resting state—the inner world of the brain, one might say metaphorically—may be one end of the bridge. The environment, the world outside the brain with its continuously changing stimuli and events, is the other end. The closer the two ends come to each other, the more likely a bridge could be constructed and mental features such as consciousness and sense of self generated. In short, mental features result from the construction of a bridge between environment and brain—and it is this bridge that is broken in the case of John and Lucie. In their vegetative (or minimally conscious) states they have no consciousness, no awareness of the contents of their environment, no bridge from their inner to their outer worlds.

Unity of Mind versus Disunity of Brain

Philosophers are much concerned with *metaphysics*, namely, determining what exists and is real, independent of our observation and sensory knowledge. Historically, most philosophers have associated the various mental features with the existence and reality of what they call a mind (or soul). Most importantly, the existence and reality of the mind are supposed to be different from the existence and reality of the body and its physical features. How, then, is the supposed existence and reality of the mind related to the existence and reality of the brain?

Descartes assumed that mind and body reflect different substances: The mind is a mental substance, whereas the body is a physical substance. These substances interact with each other, though, with the brain taking on a central role; hence the term *interactive substance dualism* that has been given to his position (Descartes et al., 1996; Northoff, 2014b, 2014c, 2014d). How might mind and body interact? Descartes believed the brain is the point where the body and the mind come into closest contact with each other. More specifically, he thought the body and the mind could interact via a little structure in the brain located beneath the ventricles—the epiphysis or pineal gland. Why the pineal gland? Descartes was aware that the brain had two hemispheres and could therefore not be considered a complete and comprehensive unity. This nonunity of the brain is important for our purposes because it contrasts with the mind, and more specifically with our mental states. More often than not, we consider our mental states or consciousness to be unified and not split into two halves like the brain.

How can we reconcile the disunity of the brain with the unity of the mind? Descartes thought that we needed to look for structures in the brain that were not present in both hemispheres and were thus not replicated. The pineal gland met this criterion, and Descartes thought it was the perfect structure to allow for direct interaction between the brain and the supposedly unitary character of mind and consciousness—the meeting place between the mind and the body. But how can two entities as disparate as the mind and the body interact with each other within the brain, or more specifically, its pineal gland? How can a nonphysical substance that defies physical laws and causality interact with something completely physical?

Descartes was confronted with the problem of how to link the mind and the brain together despite what seemed like their principally different natures. His characterization of the mind and the body by the different substances—mental and physical—explicates what I introduced as *substance dualism*, and his assumption of direct interaction between the mind and the body in the pineal gland of the brain specifies his position as *interactive dualism*.

Why are Descartes and his interactive substance dualism of the mind and the brain still important for the mind–brain discussion in our time? Descartes's characterization of the mind and the body/brain set up the framework for the contemporary discussion of the mind–brain relationship. How do we characterize the existence and reality of mental functions such as consciousness and their relation to the brain and its neuronal states? As noted previously, contemporary philosophers such as David Chalmers (Chalmers, 1996) speak of the "hard problem": Why and how is there consciousness rather than nonconsciousness? Given that we cannot see any consciousness, let alone a self, when we scan brain activity using fMRI, this is indeed puzzling. Nothing in the brain itself shows any traces of consciousness. The 19th-century German philosopher Arthur Schopenhauer said it was nothing but a "pure grey pulpy mass" (1818/1966a, 1819/1966b). Despite all the fancy imaging techniques we now have to visualize the brain and its neural activity, this characterization of the brain remains equally true.

So how does this "pure grey pulpy mass" bring forth something as colorful and complex as consciousness and our sense of self? We observe neuronal states, but not mental states, in our brain scans. We experience mental features such as consciousness, but do not experience neuronal activity. Each side leaves out the other. There seems to be a gap. We need to bridge that gap in order to understand how neuronal activity can be transformed into mental features. How can we bridge that gap? For that, let us have a closer look at the brain itself and how it is conceived in neuroscience.

Extrinsic and Cognitive View of the Brain

What exactly is the brain, and how does it operate? Neuroscience emerged around the turn of the 20th century, resulting in several different views of the brain. One view, favored by the British neurologist Sir Charles Sherrington (1857–1952), assumed the brain to be primarily reflexive in function, reacting in predefined and automatic ways to stimuli from the outside world. He believed that extrinsic stimuli almost completely and exclusively determine the activity in the brain, which is thus driven by the momentary demands of the environment. One of his students, T. Graham Brown, suggested an opposite view: that the activity of the brain is driven by *intrinsic* activity within the brain itself. Extrinsic stimuli do not cause the activity as such but rather modulate the already ongoing intrinsic activity, according to Brown. These two contrasting views of the brain and its functions prevail today.

The dichotomy of viewpoints has recently seen a resurgence within the context of functional brain imaging (see Raichle, 2010). Cognitive neuroscience researchers employ specific experimental tasks and associated stimuli to probe for changes in neural activity. The extrinsic cognitive stimuli can thereby be related to neural activity in the brain. This body of research has led to the view of a tight relationship between the neural activity of the brain and the extrinsic stimulus. Cognitive neuroscience and its more recent siblings—affective and social neuroscience—strongly rely on functional imaging, and thus seem to presuppose an extrinsic view of the brain and its function. Neural activity in the brain is consequently regarded as determined by the cognitive stimulus and demands from the extrinsic environment. Neuroscientists extend Sherrington's view of the brain as primarily reflexive with regard to sensory and motor functions into the domain of cognitive functions, such as memory and rational reasoning. Rather than responding to sensory stimuli, as in Sherrington's view, the brain is now seen as passively and automatically (i.e., reflexively) reacting to cognitive stimuli and demands from the environment. The approach may be described as an extrinsic and cognitive view of the brain. Figure 1.1a illustrates this perspective.

Intrinsic and Resting-State Views of the Brain

This extrinsic and cognitive view of the brain has been challenged by results from functional imaging. Studies by Raichle and colleagues (2001) showed that the brain is active not only when we stimulate it extrinsically and observe the associated changes—that is, *stimulus-induced activity*—but it is also active when we rest. Even when we rest,

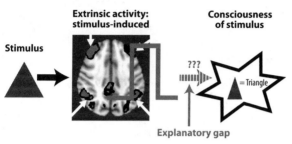

Extrinsic activity:
stimulus-induced

Consciousness
of stimulus

Stimulus

Explanatory gap

Figure 1.1a _____

without any specific extrinsic stimulation, our brain is still active and shows high resting-state activity. During the night when we sleep, our brain is not really at rest, but rather active with dreams. Sleep is rest for us. This is probably due to the fact that our brain does not sleep and is never at rest. No rest for the brain, not even in its resting state. If the resting state were true rest, you would be "at rest" even in a vegetative state without any mental features, as in the case of John and Lucie.

How does the brain maintain the never-resting activity that we, as scientists, paradoxically call a *resting state*? Activity requires energy. Our brain is energy-hungry even in the resting state. Though comprising only 2% of the body's mass, the resting brain consumes 20% of the body's total oxygen. Oxygen is essential for any kind of neuronal activity, and the brain's abundant use of the body's oxygen during rest indicates that something important must be going on (Raichle, 2009, 2010). How about the vegetative state? Maybe there is simply not enough energy in Lucie's and John's brains to sustain neuronal activity—for example, the energy-hungry resting state of the brain.

What does the brain do with this huge amount of energy in the resting state? It spends only a tiny fraction processing external stimuli, around 2–10% of its total energy budget. What happens to the rest of that energy? We do not yet know. One could consider the high resting-state activity of the brain as mere noise in the background of stimulus-induced activity. In that case the resting-state activity has no function at all; it would be irrelevant, like the background noise of the wind when playing a guitar in the park. What matters instead for the functioning of the brain is the stimulus-induced activity itself that then can be considered "the real thing." But why then does the brain waste so much energy and effort for mere noise? Do John's and Lucie's brains lose the ability to generate consciousness if they don't get enough energy?

There must be more to the resting-state activity of the brain, though this "more" remains unclear. If there is more to resting-state activity than generating mere background noise, it must somehow affect stimulus-induced activity, with the latter being dependent upon the former. Hence there must be what is called a *rest–stimulus interaction* (Northoff, Qin, & Nakao, 2010). Roughly, the concept of rest–stimulus interaction describes the mechanisms by means of which the extrinsic stimulus from the environment interacts with the ongoing intrinsic activity in the brain. Put in a converse way, taking the viewpoint of the brain itself, rest–stimulus interaction describes how the resting-state activity impacts and ingrains itself upon the neural activity changes induced by the extrinsic stimuli the brain encounters from the environment. As in daily life, during the interaction between two people, there may be various ways and multiple outcomes regarding how the brain's resting state interacts with the ongoing extrinsic stimuli.

For instance, our perception and the contents of our environment that it targets are constrained and predetermined by the level of neural activity immediately prior to the arrival of the respective stimuli. Do we perceive one and the same picture as either a grandmother or a vase? Looking at the visual cortex of your brain and its ongoing activity immediately prior to the exposure to the picture will predict whether you will perceive the grandmother or a vase. Hence, your perception and its contents do not depend only on what is presented—the extrinsic stimuli—but also the state of your brain—its resting-state activity. Figure 1.1b illustrates this point.

Although many issues about the brain's resting-state activity remain unresolved at this point in time, it is clear that it offers a view of the brain different from the extrinsic and cognitive one dominating cognitive neuroscience. The resting-state activity is an intrinsic activity of the brain that cannot be traced back to any activity occurring outside of the brain, whether in the body or the environment. This basic reality suggests the validity of an intrinsic view of the brain and its functions, like the one proposed by Brown at the beginning of the 20th century.

Such an intrinsic view can no longer be coupled specifically with cognitive functions. If the intrinsic activity of the brain exerts its impact on stimulus-induced activity, it should do so on all functions, including sensory, motor, cognitive, and affective functions. Cognitive functions might then be based not only on sensory functions but even more so on the intrinsic activity of the brain, that is, resting state and rest–stimulus interaction. This means that the extrinsic

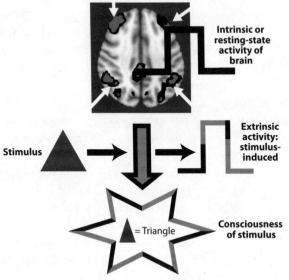

Figure 1.1b _____

and cognitive-based view of the brain in cognitive neuroscience may need to be replaced by an intrinsic and resting-state-based view of the brain.

Which view is more plausible given the data, and whether the two views of the brain can and must be linked, remain to be investigated and are among the main research themes today. The resting-state activity of the brain is the floor upon which the various kinds of furniture—that is, the different social, cognitive, affective, and sensorimotor functions—are placed. Without a floor, no furniture can be brought into the otherwise empty room. Without the resting state, no mental features can be brought in and constructed within the otherwise purely neuronal room of the brain. Why and how does the resting state accomplish this transformation?

What Do We Know?

Where does consciousness come from? Our case example demonstrates that we cannot take consciousness for granted: We could lose it easily, as the example of Lucie and John demonstrates. Consciousness, in the hands of philosophers, has primarily been attributed to the mind. Descartes's famous sentence "I think, therefore I am" also raises the question of consciousness. Since thinking (at least in Descartes's time) implied consciousness, the same sentence could have also been formulated as "I am conscious, therefore I am" which, similarly, would have led Descartes to assume the existence and reality of a mind separate from the brain.

Consciousness has been a central topic in philosophy since the ancient Greeks and especially since Descartes (Descartes et al., 1996), and it is well reflected in philosophy of mind. However, consciousness also emerged as a topic in psychology, with the American psychologist William James (1842–1910) playing a central role in that emergence. James characterized consciousness as a continuous flow or stream that structures and shapes our subjective experience (e.g., as the river's moving water makes the movement of boats possible). James's views led to the empirical investigation of consciousness in psychology at the beginning of the 20th century.

At the same time, neuroscience was just about to take off. However, rather than focusing on consciousness, neuroscience focused mainly on sensorimotor functions and their neural correlates. Consciousness was considered a nontopic—too speculative and regarded as either non-existent (as in behaviorism) or inaccessible by experimental investigation. Why? Consciousness is subjective by nature. It concerns our subjective experience, our first-person perspective, which cannot be shared by anybody else. It seems to be private and nonobservable by others. Since science, including neuroscience, relies on objective observation from a third-person perspective, it can't investigate any subjective feature that is accessible only in first-person perspective. Hence, for methodological (and often also for metaphysical) reasons, consciousness as a topic did not enter the field of neuroscience until the last 10–20 years.

How did the topic of consciousness finally enter the purview of neuroscience? One cornerstone was the introduction of functional brain imaging techniques such as PET (positron emission tomography) and fMRI, which made it possible to objectively observe subjective processes, such as measuring the neural activity of the brain while a person is dreaming. All kinds of tricky experiments have been conducted in the last two decades in search of the neural mechanisms of those contents that we consciously experience, as distinguished from the ones our brains process but of which we are not conscious. Several studies (for an overview, see chapters 18 and 19 in Northoff 2014c), for example, present visual stimuli such as a checkerboard pattern in a very weak configuration and color so that subjects respond at no more than chance levels to the question of whether they saw the pattern or not. Despite the absence of conscious recognition (on the behavioral level as reflected in the chance responses), there is nevertheless some change in neural activity that can be observed during the presentation of the stimulus indicating that it must nevertheless have been processed (in an unconscious way).

Another avenue for this investigation is studying patients like John and Lucie who lose consciousness and are in a state of unresponsive wakefulness or a vegetative state; investigations of the brains of people in these states have yielded much information about the neural mechanisms of consciousness, specifically the level or arousal needed for consciousness to occur. The destruction of the bridge between neuronal activity and mental features in John and Lucie can tell us how the neuronal–mental transformation must work in the conscious person, just as the breakdown of a bridge can reveal the mechanisms of its construction. The abnormal state reveals the normal state: how and why the bridge can serve as bridge—from destruction to construction, from the unwell brain to the healthy mind. This is the direction we take in this book to understand the neuronal–mental bridge.

What Don't We Know?

Despite all the empirical investigations with elegant and clever experimental designs, we are still unclear about why and how consciousness can emerge from the neural activity of the brain. The colorful images of the brain that PET, fMRI, and EEG provide us with don't tell us anything about the subjective features—the qualia (the "what it is like" or experiential aspect) and intentionality (the focus of the mental state directed toward certain mental contents)—that signify consciousness. There seems to be a gap between the objective features via the neural activity we observe in the brain and the subjective features of experience that we associate with consciousness. Philosophers speak of an explan-atory gap: Neuroscientific explanations of the brain's neural activity do not offer any information about consciousness and its subjective (or phenomenal) features. We may be able to map the contents of our conscious experience, such as a par-ticular face we see, in the neural activity of certain regions or networks of the brain. However, we currently have no idea why or how the neural activity of the brain brings forth these subjective features of consciousness.

We also do not know about the neuronal features in the brain that could tell us whether John and Lucie will wake up or not. Certain levels of white blood cells or sugar, for instance, tell us whether we can recover from infection or diabetes. Analogous measures are missing in the case of the vegetative and unresponsive brain. We currently do not know which of the various neuronal measures can predict whether these patients will eventually wake up. However, recent results are promising, as we will see in the next chapter. We will see that it is the resting state and some of its neuronal measures that may provide such predictive markers. The level and activity of the resting state may pro-vide the key to predict whether a patient will wake up or not: If the resting state is too low, the chance of waking up is rather low as well.

The resting state and its activity are central for con-sciousness in general. Without a proper resting state there can be no consciousness or any other mental features such as sense of self. So take a rest and consider the relevance of the resting state of your brain for your various mental fea-tures. The resting state may hold the key to the question of how neuronal activity is transformed into mental features. Specifically, there may be certain yet unknown neuronal features hidden in the resting condition that are associated with consciousness. As an analogy, the foundation of a building contains certain features that make it possible for the rest of the house—the walls and subsequent foundation—to stand on it and to carry their weight. If, in contrast, the foundation is weak, the whole house would crumble into bits. What holds for the foundation of a house applies analogously to the resting state of the brain. On the basis of some yet unclear neuronal features, the resting-state activity of the brain can assign the merely neuronal, stimulus-induced activity with mental features such as consciousness and self. The foundation transforms mere walls into a house; similarly, the resting state of the brain transforms mere neural signals into mental activity, the house of consciousness. This book is about the house of consciousness and how it is erected on the foundation of the brain's resting-state activity and how changes in the latter impact the former.

Chapter 2

CONSCIOUSNESS

—————— PREVIEW ——————

**What are the mechanisms of
neuronal–mental transformations?**

Recall John and Lucie, whose motorcycle crash put them,
and more specifically their brains, into a vegetative state
(John) and minimally conscious state (Lucie): John showed
no reaction, no movement, and no communication, whereas
Lucie yielded minimal signs of all three. As outsiders we
would say that they lost consciousness, but how can we
specify exactly what they lost? We can determine what they
lost and what is wrong in their brain. This information, in
turn, reveals insight into those neural mechanisms in the
healthy brain that transform merely neuronal states into
conscious states. The focus in this chapter is to reveal these
mechanisms of neuronal–mental transformation by learning
from their *absence* in vegetative states or minimal presence
in minimally conscious states (MCS).

Inactive Consciousness and Its Active Brain

Clinicians speak of a level of consciousness defined by
arousal: John's and Lucie's levels of arousal are so low that

they do not show any signs of what we could refer to as experience or behavior. Patients in an unresponsive wakefulness state or vegetative state (UWS/VS) can still open their eyes but cannot respond to any external stimuli, as noted previously. Those in comas have closed eyes; their level of consciousness is consequently extremely low, even lower than those in UWS/VS, which in turn is lower than those in MCS. This is also true of how you may have felt in that boring meeting earlier this week, when you dozed off for a minute. When you sleep during the night, your level of consciousness is very low, and it increases when you wake up.

Consciousness appears to be absent, if we can say that, when its level is low. However, as the British-Canadian researcher Adrian Owen and his Belgian colleague Steven Laureys (Monti et al., 2010; Owen et al., 2006) discovered, absence does not prevent the brain from still being active. Owen and Laureys investigated unresponsive patients in vegetative states similar to those of John and Lucie (see Chapter 1); their patients did not show any reaction to the environment and were considered nonconscious. This type of VS can occur in the wake of trauma and brain lesions, as in, for instance, motor bikers who suffered an accident.

What did Owen and Laureys do with these patients? They put them into a scanner for an fMRI and gave them specific instructions on a screen: either to imagine playing tennis or to imagine navigating the various rooms of their own house. When imagining these tasks, healthy subjects show activity in those regions of the brain that are involved in the execution of playing tennis—the sensorimotor cortex—and house navigation—the parietal cortex and the hippocampus.

What about patients in vegetative states, like John and

Lucie? Despite appearing nonconscious and nonresponsive, the same regions still activated in them as in healthy subjects when instructed to perform these tasks (via screen). This finding has been replicated in other studies. In some cases, the patients were even able to indicate answers to specific questions by associating "Yes" with tennis playing and "No" with house navigation. What do these results tell us about consciousness? First and foremost the data tell us that some patients with VS may still have cognitive abilities. But does this imply that these patients are still *conscious*? There is much debate today whether patients with VS have some preserved islands of consciousness that activate the respective regions in the brain and allow them to perform these imaginary tasks.

The occurrence of cognitive functions in patients with VS like John and Lucie cannot be denied because it is well reflected in their neural activity during the imaginary tasks. But does that activation really imply consciousness? Many people think so because a certain level of consciousness is necessary in order to follow the instruction (and produce the kind of activity observed). However, alternatively, one may also claim that the stimuli themselves—independent of whether the patients recognize them or not—induce the kind of neural activity pattern Adrian Owen observed in his brain scans. There may be cognitive processing without consciousness—and, indeed, this possibility is supported empirically by the fact that the degree of stimulus-induced activity (during visual–spatial and motor imagery, as described above) did not predict the level of consciousness as clinically measured.

Is the Self Vegetative Too?

Does this research imply that stimulus-induced activity can be dissociated from consciousness? Could the navigation of a house and its underlying neural activity occur unconsciously? If that were the case, then the ability to navigate the house would not indicate the presence of consciousness. But might it indicate the presence of a self as dissociated from consciousness?

Our research group studied several patients with VS (Huang, Dai, et al., 2014; Huang, Wang, et al., 2014; Huang, Zhang, Wu, & Northoff, 2014; Qin & Northoff, 2011). Rather than applying purely cognitive stimuli, as Owen and Laureys did (Monti et al., 2010; Owen et al., 2006), we used self-specific stimuli such as the patient's name or autobiographical events to induce brain activity—asking John about his love of motorcycles, for example. Surprisingly, patients with VS were well able to differentiate self- and non-self-specific stimuli, as indicated by their neuronal activity, specifically in the midline regions. Those are the regions in the middle of the brain that seem to have a special role in self-specific stimulus processing (I discuss this process at greater length in Chapter 8). Most interestingly, unlike the other studies using cognitive stimulation, the degree of self-related activity predicted the degree of consciousness: The better the patients were able to make the neuronal distinction between self- and non-self-specific stimuli, the higher their level of consciousness.

Accordingly, self-related activity may indeed be special in both senses: mentally and clinically. Mentally, self-related activity may be central for constituting our sense of self, the experience that we are one and the same person. At the same time it may be associated with consciousness in a yet unclear way that may be clinically relevant, in that it allows us to predict the actual level of consciousness and possibly also therapeutic recovery.

Do self and self-specificity play a special role in consciousness? We currently do not know. Past and present philosophers such as Descartes and Nagel assumed that the self is central to consciousness: Without self or subject, the philosophers like to say, there can be no consciousness; there needs to be a self or subject who experiences consciousness, whereas the absence of such a self makes any experience impossible. But do our findings in UWS/VS support that assumption? Before we can answer this question, we need more neuroscientific findings about self-consciousness in both healthy people and in patients with UWS/VS, as well as more careful philosophical elaboration of the concepts of self, consciousness, and self-consciousness.

These studies of patients with VS opened some fascinating questions about the self's relation to consciousness that we'll continue to examine in this chapter. Why and how can self-specific contents be better processed than non-self-specific stimuli in these patients' brains? Is there a self buried somewhere in the brain? That leads us to the question of how the brain can assign consciousness to contents such as self- and non-self-specific stimuli. In addition to the level of consciousness, then, we need to discuss a second dimension of consciousness—its contents.

The Subjective Character of Consciousness

Everybody knows what it is to be conscious. You experience it continuously during the day when you are awake. When reading this book, for instance, and specifically these lines, you are conscious of the contents written here—the words, the sentences, and their meaning. More specifically, you perceive this book in a conscious mode, perhaps feeling certain emotions like frustration and anger at a seemingly banal beginning. And you become conscious of your own thoughts and cognitions tempting you to contradict the definitions given here, or to move on to something more gripping. Ultimately, even one's own self—the one who reads these lines—enters consciousness, yielding what is called *self-consciousness*.

Consciousness is such a basic human phenomenon that any definition seems superfluous. However, if we want to understand how consciousness is produced, we need to determine what it is for which we are searching. Otherwise we remain blind about our direction.

So what is consciousness? Let me first give a tentative definition. The philosopher Thomas Nagel (1974) characterized consciousness as having a "what it is like" quality. The concept of "what it is like" describes this experience, and thus consciousness goes along with a particular quality, a phenomenological, qualitative feeling described as *qualia*. You experience the redness of the book's red letters in terms of this feeling; you have a quale of the letters' red color. You may just perceive or observe the red color. In contrast, you do not experience a particular quality; the red color is purely quantitative. That changes once you switch from your third-person mode of observation to a first-person mode of experience. Now you experience the color as part of your own self, and you experience the feeling of the redness of the cover. This is the moment when philosophers like to speak of qualia. Hence, the phenomenological, qualitative feeling, the qualia, must be regarded as a hallmark of experience and thus of consciousness.

Imagine you like eating chocolate. You see the chocolate in the store and start to develop an urge or craving. You buy the chocolate and taste it piece by piece. You enjoy the chocolate. Especially bitter chocolate is your favorite. You enjoy and dwell in the bitterness of the taste; this is your subjective experience. Your experience of the bitterness in the taste of the chocolate goes way beyond its merely objective features. The bitterness is your subjective experience of the objectively bitter chocolate. Since you love bitter chocolate so much, you may subjectively experience the bitterness in your first-person perspective to a much stronger degree than it is objectively present in the chocolate itself (independent of your tasting the same chocolate). There is thus a "what it is like" for you to experience and taste the bitterness of the chocolate.

Consciousness, in this sense, is subjective and private rather than objective and public. Due to its subjective and private character, consciousness cannot be observed by others. Nor can we observe it in the brain, where we see nothing but neural activity, not qualia or experience. Observing changes in the brain's neural activity provides some clues, but what remains unclear is how, why, and when this neural activity, which is purely nonconscious by itself, is transformed into a conscious state. Hence the old problem: The quest for neuronal–mental transformation is specified and condensed in the question of why and how neuronal states yield conscious contents.

Conscious versus Unconscious Contents

How then can neuroscientists research consciousness? One starting point is the content of consciousness. For example, we are conscious of the book in front of us and its red-colored letters. The book is thus the content of consciousness, also known as the phenomenal content. Consciousness always has contents. These contents can include events, persons, or objects in the environment. Alternatively, the contents of consciousness can also consist of our own thoughts or some imaginary scene involving persons, objects, or events in our dreams when we sleep—like John, from our case example in the first chapter, picturing that first motorcycle ride with Lucie before everything went wrong.

Phenomenal contents must be considered as one central dimension of consciousness. Since they lost consciousness, John and Lucie can apparently no longer experience anything at all; they do not seem to have any phenomenal contents anymore because their brains provide them with no access to the phenomenal contents. If one no longer experiences phenomenal contents, one does not react anymore and therefore shows no behavior. That is why John and Lucie are in vegetative states that are also characterized by unresponsiveness.

These phenomenal contents can now be taken as the starting point for neuroscientific investigation. Neuroscientists can investigate the neuronal differences between contents that are conscious and those that remain unconscious. How can we further illustrate this difference? The unconscious content may still exert an impact on behavior: For instance, you avoid going on bridges because, as a young child, you fell down from a bridge and broke your right leg.

When avoiding bridges as an adult, you may not be aware that an event in your past makes you avoid that path in the forest. However, it's possible for this unconscious content to become conscious and for you to realize that it is because of your earlier experience that you avoid crossing bridges. Another example: Should John ever emerge from his vegetative state, he may avoid motorcycles at all costs, even if he can't remember exactly why.

These examples illustrate that the same content— whether a particular event, person, or object—can be presented in both a conscious mode with subjective experience and in an unconscious mode. The neuronal difference between the conscious and the unconscious mode must then be related to consciousness—what we neuroscientists can expect is a more accurate measurement than MacDougall's 21-gram soul. This neuronal difference is what I mean when I use the term *neural correlates of consciousness*. Where do the contents of consciousness come from and what are their neural correlates? One may now want to argue that they originate from our senses and the sensory functions of the brain. For instance, color is processed by the brain's visual system whereas the processing of chocolate is related to the gustatory and olfactory systems. Are consciousness and its contents thus nothing more than the products of the brain's sensory functions? Earlier philosophers such as David Hume and many current-day philosophers and neuroscientists do indeed assume that conscious contents are derived from the brain's sensory functions. However, these sensory functions only allow for the processing of the sensory contents themselves—for example, the stimuli related to the color red and the sight, feel, and taste of the chocolate. In contrast, sensory processing itself does not explain the specifically subjective component, the "what it is like," that is associated with and characterizes the conscious experience of these contents. Hence, an additional neuronal process is needed to account for the neural correlates of consciousness. Let's explore some past and current theories of what these additional processes, the neural correlates, may be.

The Cyclic Processing of Contents

Gerald Edelman is an American neuroscientist who was awarded a Nobel Prize for his work in immunology and his discoveries concerning the mechanisms operating in the immune system. The immune system is in charge of producing biochemical substances that protect and defend the body from foreign and potentially dangerous substances. After he discovered the immunological code, Edelman, much like Francis Crick (who co-discovered the double helix of DNA), turned to the brain in the hopes of revealing the neural code of consciousness (Edelman, 2003, 2005). Edelman considers cyclic processing, or circularity, within the neural organization of the brain as central to consciousness. Cyclic processing describes a chain of processing with different cycles wherein one and the same stimulus can be processed multiple times and thereby elaborated and integrated with other stimuli. Specifically, it concerns the reentrance of neural activity in the same region after looping and circulating through other regions in reentrant (or feedback) circuits.

Let me describe the different regions of such cyclic processing for visual stimuli to make Edelman's theory less abstract. The primary visual cortex (V1) is the first entrance point for visual stimuli in the cortex of the brain.

The initial neural activity in V1 is transferred to subsequent or higher visual regions, such as the inferior temporal (IT) cortex, in feed-forward connections. These regions further elaborate the visual stimuli and process them in more complex ways by, for instance, linking the incoming stimuli to other visual stimuli. From there, the stimuli are conveyed to the thalamus, a subcortical region, which relays the information back to V1 and the other cortical regions. This "route" implies what is described as thalamic–cortical reentrant connections, a cyclic process involving different regions in the brain.

At what point in this cyclic process does consciousness emerge? Edelman assumes that the multiple and circular processing of stimuli in these different regions makes possible the assignment of consciousness. Why and how such circular feedback processing assigns consciousness (i.e., mental features) to the otherwise purely neuronal activity remains unclear. How would we experience this feedback cycle and how does it relate to our consciousness? Imagine that you initially perceive some kind of little animal walking nearby in the park, but you are not sure whether it is a cat or a small dog. Milliseconds later you perceive the same scene in a clearer way and your cognitions tell you that the animal is a cat. Then you might quickly compare this cat in the park to your own cat, worrying, "Is that *my* cat? Did my cat escape? Did I leave open the door?"

The fur you initially perceived and the animal you then recognized as a cat are put into different and novel contexts. This means that the neuronal activity related to your recognition of the animal as a cat must reenter other regions in the brain, which then send feedback loops to the original regions that were activated during your initial perception of the fur-coated animal. In the context of this theory, one may assume that John and Lucie seemed to no longer possess such reentrance and feedback loops. In their case, the contents are processed but no longer reenter in different contexts. The contents are processed only once or twice instead of multiple times, as in the conscious brain. Although direct experimental proof of such feedback or reentrant processing remains elusive, indirect measurement of, for instance, the electrical traces of the stimuli in the brain, as measured by EEG, lend support to such an assumption (see Northoff, 2014c, Chapters 18 and 19).

The Integration of Contents and Information

What is the purpose of Edelman's feedback circuits? To integrate information. This concept led Giulio Tononi (2012; Tononi & Koch, 2015), an Italian researcher and former student of Edelman, to emphasize the integration of information as a central neuronal mechanism in yielding consciousness. He developed what he called the *integrated information theory* (IIT). The IIT postulates that the degree to which information is linked and integrated in the brain is central to the production of consciousness. The integration of information can, for instance, be achieved by establishing *functional connectivity* between different regions' neural activities. Increased functional connectivity between these regions may allow us to link and integrate more information of different types. If, in contrast, functional connectivity between the different regions is low or disrupted, the information from these regions can no longer be integrated. Tononi assumes that low information integration makes consciousness impossible.

How does Tononi support his assumption? He investigated various disorders of consciousness, including the vegetative state, as well as naturally occurring variations in consciousness that occur during sleep (especially NREM sleep) and the intentional reduction of consciousness via anesthesia; all of these states are characterized by reduced or absent consciousness, whatever their cause. Despite the differences in the origin of the loss of consciousness, all three categories exhibited reduced functional connectivity throughout the brain, and in particular, in the thalamic–cortical reentrant connections. The individuals all showed decreased information integration, which Tononi assumes to be central in their decrease in consciousness (see Tononi, 2012, for summary).

Why are the thalamic–cortical reentrant connections so central to consciousness? These connections process all kinds of stimuli, independent of their origin and their associated contents. According to Tononi, they allow the brain to generate particular qualia, which can then be associated with the various contents and become conscious. Returning to our previously cited examples, such qualia may consist of the bitterness you taste when eating your preferred chocolate or the redness of the red-colored letters you experience when looking at your book. Hence, what Nagel describes as the "what it is like" quality may be accounted for neuronally by the integration of information in the brain.

If, in contrast, the functional connectivity, and thus the thalamic–cortical reentrant processing is low or completely disrupted, the contents can no longer be associated with qualia. Consequently, the addition of the specific quality, the qualia, remains impossible, rendering it also impossible for the contents to achieve consciousness. The redness of the book's cover in front of you is no longer a phenomenal content; there is no experience of it and hence no consciousness at all.

Let us come back to our cat example. Each step in the description involves an integration of different kinds of information. First you just perceive mere fur, and then you integrate that information with a specific shape, the shape of the cat as distinguished from the shape of a dog. Then you start comparing this cat with your own cat and integrate information about both cats. That then leads you to integrate the information about your cat with information about your house when you start thinking about whether you left the door open. Plenty of integration is going on here. Tononi argues that such integration of different types of information makes consciousness possible. In this viewpoint, John and Lucie lost consciousness when their brains lost the ability, due to injury, to integrate different types content or information.

Contents of Consciousness Become Global

Neuroscientists such as Baars (2005) and Dehaene (Dehaene & Changeux, 2011; Dehaene, Charles, King, & Marti, 2014) also address the question of the neural correlates of consciousness. They proposed a global distribution of neural activity across many brain regions in a "global workspace" that is central for yielding consciousness. The single stimulus itself and its local processing in specific regions of the brain such as the sensory cortex cannot explain consciousness, they contended. There must be something more happening in the brain beyond its local processing in order to make consciousness possible. This "something more" consists of the global distribution of the information and its contents across the whole brain in order for them to become associated with consciousness. If information is only processed locally, within particular regions but not globally throughout the whole brain, it cannot be associated with consciousness, according to Baars and Dehaene.

The main distinction between unconsciousness and consciousness is then assumed to be manifested in the difference between the local and the global distribution of neural activity. Hence, the global distribution of neural activity is considered a sufficient condition, and thus the neural correlate, of consciousness. Deheane and Changeux (2011) proposed what they describe as a "global neuronal workspace theory." A set of regions that is not limited to specific sensory stimuli (e.g., the visual cortex) must be involved. At the same time this set of regions must be linked to all other regions and networks in the brain. The researchers identified such regions in the prefrontal and parietal networks in the brain and assume that this prefrontal–parietal connection must be recruited by the stimulus to allow the global processing of the stimulus, which in turn assigns consciousness to it.

How, though, does the prefrontal–parietal network assign consciousness to a stimulus? The stimulus is first processed locally, in specific sensory regions of the brain: The visual stimulus, such as the color red of the book title's letters, is processed in the visual cortex, whereas the chocolate and its taste are processed in gustatory and olfactory cortices. However, processing does not stop here. The stimulus is processed in other regions of the brain and ultimately it may reach the prefrontal and parietal cortices. If the stimulus reaches the prefrontal and parietal cortices, it may or may not induce some activity there. The prefrontal and parietal cortices may have a say here: They may either open or close their doors, so to speak, to the processing of the stimulus. The "doors" here consist of the level of resting-state activity in the prefrontal and parietal networks: If there is too much activity, the stimulus cannot be processed and the prefrontal–parietal doors remain closed—which in turn means that the door of consciousness will not be open to the stimulus. If, in contrast, the prefrontal–parietal activity level is just right, the stimulus can induce activity changes and be processed globally and, therefore, be related to consciousness. Accordingly, the prefrontal–parietal networks serve as the gatekeepers that "decide" whether the hitherto locally processed stimulus can be globalized throughout the whole brain. Globalization in this context amounts to consciousness (or, analogously, to phenomenalization), whereas the lack of globalization results in the absence of consciousness, with mere unconscious or preconscious processing of the stimulus taking place.

How about our fur and cat example? *Fur* and *cat* go global when they are linked to and integrated within the context of the perceiver's house. The scope of contents to which they are linked is more and more extended and finally integrated into a global workspace where all contents come together. The global workspace can be compared to the cooking point in which you, as cook, put all the ingredients together. John and Lucie seem to still be able to process the single ingredients, but apparently their brains no longer provide the cooking pot, the global workspace, wherein everything can be put together and boiled. This scenario is indeed supported by findings of reduced activity in exactly these prefrontal and parietal networks in patients with VS. One may consequently assume that the prefrontal–parietal global neuronal workspace in these patients is no longer properly recruited and activated during the processing of extrinsic stimuli.

The Level of Consciousness in the Resting State

What in the brain decides whether a given stimulus gains access to the various regions and networks, including the global workspace? Earlier philosophers such as Descartes assumed that the mind interfaces with the brain (as in the little pineal gland; see above) and "decides" which stimuli will access the brain. His philosophical successors, such as the German philosopher Immanuel Kant in the 19th century and more contemporary philosophers such as Shawn Gallagher (2005) and Dan Zahavi (2005), assume the presence of a self or subject (as closely related to the body; Gallagher 2005) that allows or prevents access of stimuli to the brain. Today we have plenty of evidence to show that there is neither a mind nor a self or subject separate and distinct from the brain: It is the brain itself, and more specifically its intrinsic activity, that may allow or prevent environmental stimuli from being properly processed. So, it is the brain's intrinsic activity that plays a vital role in deciding whether we are conscious or unconscious.

How does the brain's intrinsic activity make this determination? Let's return to John and Lucie. In addition to the self-specific stimuli discussed above, we (Huang, Dai, et al., 2014) also investigated the resting-state activity in our patients with VS. As in previous studies, we found decreased functional connectivity and, a novel finding, decreased variability in the resting-state activity. As noted, the term *functional connectivity* refers to the "highways" in the brain along which the different regions can communicate with each other. These highways seem to be reduced in VS. *Variability* concerns the degree of change in the amplitude of activity (i.e., the degree of traffic, so to speak, and how it changes during the day). In VS, the amplitude of activity (or the degree of traffic) no longer change as much but remains more or less the same across time. The brain's resting-state activity is no longer as variable, and that means that it can no longer react to novel stimuli and adapt its activity level.

Imagine that you speak only five words of English. This paucity of words makes it hard for you to respond to other people in a flexible and adaptive way. The same seems to be the case in VS. Here the variability of the brain's resting-state activity is reduced—and that, in turn, makes it hard, if not impossible, for the resting state to react in a flexible way to different stimuli, let alone assign consciousness to them.

Most importantly, our research revealed that decreased variability in the resting-state activity of midline brain regions predicted the degree of self-specific activity observed in these patients—which, in turn, as described above, predicted the level of consciousness. Step by step. If the resting state of the brain is no longer variable, it cannot relate the extrinsic stimuli to itself—there is reduced self-specific activity. And if the stimuli's relation (i.e., self-specificity) to the resting state is reduced, they can no longer be associated with, and assigned to, a certain level of consciousness. This is what the correlations tell us. In sum, the resting-state activity, and especially its degree of variability, impacts the level of consciousness, though apparently not in a direct way, but as mediated by the degree of stimulus-induced or task-evoked activity.

To state the implications of our findings more formally: The resting-state activity may not be considered a sufficient condition of the level of consciousness—a neural correlate—but rather a neural *predisposition*. Neural *correlate* would mean that the resting state itself is directly related to the level of consciousness. However, we did not find a direct correlation between resting-state activity and level of consciousness. However, we did observe that the resting-state variability correlated with the degree of self-specific activity—which in turn predicted the level of consciousness. Hence, the resting state is indirectly related to the level of consciousness, with self-specificity as an intermediate. The higher the variability of the resting state, the higher the degree of self-specificity and the higher, in turn, the level of consciousness. Without the resting state, there would be no self-specificity, and without self-specificity, there is no consciousness. The resting state and its variability may thus be a necessary condition of the level of consciousness, though not a sufficient condition by itself. It is not a neural correlate of consciousness but rather a neural predisposition of consciousness: The resting state does not cause consciousness, but it does predispose the level of consciousness that occurs.

What are the features of the resting-state activity that predispose or make consciousness possible? How does the resting state assign a certain level of consciousness to its contents? This question concerns the mechanisms underlying the interaction between resting state and stimulus: the rest–stimulus interaction. The resting state must have certain properties that allow it to react to the stimulus in such a way that the latter can be associated with consciousness. This process is explored in the following.

The Rest–Stimulus Interaction and Consciousness

How is the rest–stimulus interaction related to consciousness? The research group around the German-French neuroscientist and neurologist Andreas Kleinschmidt investigated what is described as "bistable perception" (see Sadaghiani, Hesselmann, Friston, & Kleinschmidt, 2010, for an overview), which refers to the fluctuation between two different perceptions with regard to one and the same stimulus—for example, the ability to perceive the well-known optical illusion that depicts either a vase or an old woman. How is this bistable perception possible? Kleinschmidt and his colleagues observed that the degree of preceding resting-state activity in those regions processing the vase and the woman predicts whether one perceives the stimulus—in this case, a picture—as either a vase or the face of an old woman. If, for instance, the resting-state activity prior to the presentation of the picture is high in the region that processes faces (the fusiform face area), the subject will see the picture as an old woman. If, in contrast, preceding activity levels are high in the regions processing inanimate objects, the subject will perceive a vase rather than an old woman's face. Hence, the resting-state activity itself—its level prior to the actual stimulus—seems to be central in selecting the contents suitable for assignment to a level of consciousness.

The interaction between the resting state of the brain

and the extrinsic stimulus thus allows for interaction between the level and the content of consciousness. Specifically, the prestimulus level of resting-state activity is central in determining the level of consciousness that can possibly be assigned to the subsequent stimulus and its respective contents. The studies described above are concerned with what is described in the current literature as the neural correlates of consciousness (NCC). Because these researchers target the specific contents of consciousness, one can speak of content-NCC, and how that is related to the level of consciousness, the level-NCC.

The quest for the level-NCC implies a distinction between consciousness and unconsciousness. In contrast, Kleinschmidt and colleagues' studies (e.g., Sadaghiani et al., 2010) do not tell us anything about the distinction between consciousness and nonconsciousness—that is, the "hard problem." In order to address the latter distinction, we need to account for the temporal and spatial structure of the brain's intrinsic activity; this information may tell us why and how the brain can assign consciousness to the various contents and their extrinsic or environmental stimuli. By constituting a temporal and spatial structure, the brain's intrinsic activity can impose itself upon all extrinsic stimuli. As such, the intrinsic activity of the brain may provide a grid, template, or schemata along whose lines all subsequent forms of neural activity, intrinsic and extrinsic, are organized and structured.

That the intrinsic activity of the brain (including its connections to the rest of the nervous system) seems to provide an organizational template has already been described by the American psychologist and neuroscientist Karl Lashley (1890–1958). He said:

> A second point of major importance is that the nervous system is not a neutral medium on which learning imposes any form of organization whatsoever. On the contrary, it has definite predilections for certain forms of organization and imposes these upon the sensory impulses that reach it. In its functional organization, the nervous system seems to consist of schemata or basic patterns within which new stimuli are fitted (Lashley, 1949, p. 35).

What do I mean by *organizational template*? I am referring to a spatial and temporal structure of the brain's intrinsic activity. The spatial structure emerges from different neural networks that are constituted in the resting state. There is a network in the middle of the brain, the *default-mode network*, which is in charge of processing self-related content. A network at the edges of the brain—the executive control network—allows for cognition and action. The salience network assigns salience and relevance to stimuli, and the sensorimotor network includes various sensory and motor regions. What about the temporal structure? The resting state shows continuous change in its activity level; these changes can occur in different frequency ranges, which may or may not be coupled or linked to each other. Such coupling between different frequency ranges provides a certain temporal structure, template, or grid.

Neural Predisposition versus Neural Correlates of Consciousness

How is the spatial–temporal structure of the brain's intrinsic activity transformed into the mental features of consciousness? Well, once again we must admit that, for now, we don't know. We do know that there is a certain temporal and spatial structure to the brain's intrinsic activity; we just don't know how it's related to consciousness. One of the central phenomenal features of consciousness is spatial and temporal continuity. Your consciousness, for instance, never stops; you perceive the book in front of you, then you glance over to the bottle of wine and after that to the cheese standing on the table. Accordingly, the term *spatial and temporal continuity* refers to how contents of consciousness are always embedded in a spatial–temporal grid that provides temporal flow (continuity) and spatial integration in our experience. Instead of being segregated in time and space, the different contents are spatially and temporally linked in our consciousness.

Think of it like Owen's and Laurey's (Monti et al., 2010; Owen et al., 2006) navigational experiment: The contents of consciousness flow within the navigational grid of the patient's home. Despite their occurrence at different discrete points in physical time, we nevertheless experience a temporal continuum, a seamless transition between the different contents in our consciousness. This temporal continuum in consciousness does not seem to correspond to the objective, discrete points in time we observe in a third-person perspective. Instead, we experience a continuum between different discrete points in our consciousness and thus what phenomenally is described as "dynamic flow" (James, 1890) or "phenomenal time" (Husserl, 1913/1982).

Although there has been much debate about the nature of time and consciousness, there has been less discussion about the experience of space in consciousness. As with temporal continuity, there is also spatial continuity in our consciousness. We see, for instance, the table standing in front of us in continuation of the floor on which it is standing and contiguous with the chairs arranged around it. The contents in consciousness are not experienced at their different discrete points in physical space. Instead, they are embedded and integrated into a spatial continuum with multiple transitions between the different discrete points in physical space. As in the case of time, the contents are woven into a spatial grid or template that emphasizes continuity and transition over discontinuity and segregation.

The Form of Consciousness is Spatial–Temporal

How are a spatial–temporal grid and its spatial and temporal continuities created? One may now assume that the brain's intrinsic activity is central in constituting the spatial–temporal grid. If so, one would assume that the neuronal features underlying the spatial and temporal structure of the brain's intrinsic activity would account for the spatial and temporal features as we experience them in consciousness. In turn, one would then expect the temporal distances experienced between different contents in consciousness to correspond to the temporal distances constituted in the temporal structure of the brain's intrinsic activity.

If that is the case, then the intrinsic activity and its spatial–temporal structure provide the form or structure of consciousness. The concept of *form* refers to the structure or organization within which the various stimuli from outside the brain interact with, and are integrated within, the brain's intrinsic activity if "they want to be processed," so to speak. The intrinsic activity and its spatial–temporal structure impose themselves upon the stimuli, integrating

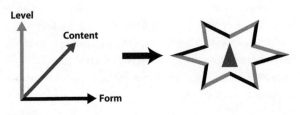

Figure 2.1a

them; and it is this integration that may make it possible to assign consciousness to the stimuli. Importantly, the intrinsic activity of the brain and its spatial–temporal structure organize the incoming sensory stimuli; the former orders and groups the latter and integrates them into its spatial–temporal grid. That integration, in turn, makes possible the assignment of consciousness to each sensory stimulus and its respective contents. Consciousness may then be conceived in a spatial–temporal way; without this spatial–temporal grid or form underlying the brain's intrinsic activity, consciousness would not be possible.

What is it that the resting state provides that makes consciousness possible? Here and in *Unlocking the Brain* (Northoff, 2014b, 2014c), I argue that the intrinsic activity and its spatial–temporal structure provide the form of consciousness. And it is this form that, first and foremost, makes possible the transformation of a purely neuronal state into a conscious or mental state. Accordingly, by providing such form, the brain's intrinsic activity and its spatial–temporal structure make possible or predispose consciousness: The form is a necessary but nonsufficient condition or neural predisposition of consciousness (NPC), rather than being sufficient by itself, as are the neural correlates of consciousness (NCC). In the case of Lucie and John, the spatial–temporal structure of their respective resting states seems to be frozen—it is not active due to lack of energy. Hence these two patients lack the form of consciousness as the NPC.

The Hard Problem with the Soft Solution

Let's return to the hard problem as raised in the first chapter. To restate: Why is there consciousness rather than nonconsciousness? The hard problem involves the mystery of what I describe as neural–mental transformation; that is, what, where, how, and why does a purely neuronal state transform into mental features that we call consciousness?

How are the brain's intrinsic activity and its suggested spatial–temporal structure related to the hard problem? The answer is clear: The brain shows intrinsic activity, which, because of its presumed spatial–temporal structure, predisposes the possible emergence of consciousness. The predisposition for possible consciousness can be transformed into the manifestation of actual consciousness by the "right" context: the "right" extrinsic stimulus and its "right" interaction with the intrinsic activity.

Although possible consciousness is supposed to be mediated by the neural predispositions, the intrinsic activity and its spatial–temporal structure, actual consciousness may be related to neural correlates. *Neural correlates* refer to the sufficient conditions of actual consciousness. Both neural predispositions and neural correlates may be related to different neuronal mechanisms that have to act in conjunction in order to constitute consciousness rather than nonconsciousness.

In short, I assume the conjunction of neural predisposi-

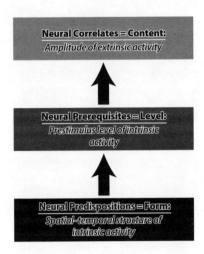

Neural Correlates = Content:
Amplitude of extrinsic activity

Neural Prerequisites = Level:
Prestimulus level of intrinsic activity

Neural Predispositions = Form:
Spatial-temporal structure of intrinsic activity

Figure 2.1b

tion and neural correlates as an empirical answer to the hard problem. Only if both go together will we be able to fully explain consciousness. The *neural predispositions* will account for the necessary conditions of possible consciousness, and the *neural correlates* will reveal the necessary and sufficient conditions of actual consciousness. This is an empirical answer to the hard problem. However, it's nothing but a soft solution for the philosopher, whose real concern is usually metaphysical issues, the hard solutions. However, even such a soft solution may nevertheless be of use to the philosopher. Why? The empirical solution sketched here may provide some clues. By pointing out the brain's intrinsic activity and its spatial–temporal structure as the neural predisposition of consciousness, we may be able to develop a different methodological approach to investigating the centuries-old mind–brain problem. It allows us, for example, to replace the mind as the methodological starting point for metaphysical mind–brain reflection with the brain and its intrinsic features. Once we are clear about these intrinsic features—namely those that define the brain as distinct from the mind and from other organs—we may investigate how the existence and reality of those intrinsic features are related metaphysically to mental features.

This short discussion shows that the consideration of the brain's intrinsic activity is not important only in empirical neuroscience terms (i.e., to understand the neural mechanisms underlying consciousness), but is also highly relevant for philosophy and the metaphysical quest for an understanding of the mind–brain relationship. In the same way the intrinsic activity changes the neuroscientific approach to consciousness, it is also a game changer in philosophy when it comes to addressing the brain–mind problem. Instead of asking the question, "How is the mind related to the brain?" we can now raise the question, "How is the brain's intrinsic activity transformed into mental features?"

The methodological starting point of philosophy is not only different here but reversed: Traditionally in philosophy we start with the mind and continue from there to the brain, whereas now we start with the brain itself, its intrinsic activity, and extend from there to mental features such as consciousness. What is described as a metaphysical problem between two different existences and realities, mind and brain, is now converted into a transformation problem: How does the intrinsic activity of the brain transform neuronal activity into mental features?

The traditional philosopher may be puzzled. He or she longs for answers to the mind–brain problem, to understand how the metaphysical existence and reality of the mind are related to the brain. I do not provide such answers. Instead, I propose an escape from the question that makes any subsequent mind–brain answer or solution futile. If there is no meaning to such a question, there can be no meaningful answer.

Is Consciousness a Basic Function of the Brain?

Traditional philosophers might now raise the question of what is going on in John's and Lucie's minds in their vegetative states. Philosophers past (e.g., Descartes, Kant) and present (e.g., Searle, Rosenthal) usually conceive of consciousness as a higher-order function that may be empirically related to cognitive functions such as memory and attention. Other philosophers (e.g., Merleau-Ponty, Thompson) emphasize the role of the body and its sensorimotor functions: Because of the body and its sensorimotor functions, we are based or located in, and in continuous contact with, the world—which in turn makes consciousness possible. Without any such location and contact with the world, no cognitive function would be able to generate consciousness. Hence, so say the advocates of this position, we need to consider the body and its sensorimotor function as the most central condition of consciousness. Rather than "locating" consciousness in the higher-order functions of our cognition, consciousness must be associated with lower-order functions such as perception and motor behavior (action).

The findings and hypothesis sketched here seem to be even more radical. Is consciousness a basic and fundamental function of the brain's resting state? I think it is. Since the brain's resting-state activity is ongoing, it occurs prior to and independent of the instantiation of sensorimotor and cognitive function. Therefore consciousness can neither be conceived as a higher-order cognitive function nor as a lower-order sensorimotor function. Instead, like the brain's resting state that provides the basis for any subsequent stimulus-induced activity, consciousness provides the foundation for any subsequent sensorimotor and cognitive functions. We must wait, though, for future empirical data to see whether they support such a view of consciousness as a function of the resting state's spatial–temporal structure.

If this new perspective were supported empirically, we would need to radically reconceptualize our view of consciousness. Rather than looking upward to our higher-order functions, we would instead look downward to our brain's resting-state activity. Deep down in the brain itself, in its intrinsic activity, we can find the origin or source of consciousness, its neural predisposition. We should not let ourselves become confused by the colorful forms of stimulus-induced activity as related to the various sensorimotor and cognitive functions of the brain. They are nothing but a specification of consciousness that is already predisposed by the resting state itself and its spatial–temporal structure. Accordingly, to trace down consciousness in the brain, we must understand the spatial–temporal structure of its intrinsic activity. What must the spatial–temporal structure look like in order to predispose consciousness? This question is discussed in the next chapter.

Chapter 3

THE SELF

John and Lucie are lying in their hospital beds, unresponsive. Family and friends come and go, sitting bedside, sometimes talking, recounting old times and shared experiences. They leave flowers and cards containing messages that reference specific moments or feelings that John and Lucie would understand and appreciate. In short, the visitors all address a specific self—the John or the Lucie they know and remember. But in their vegetative states, do Lucie and John still show any signs of a self? Are they still subjects who experience something, or are they mere objects, blending in more and more with their hospital beds? How does consciousness relate to the self? Is consciousness necessary for a sense of self?

The Nature of the Self

We can begin by asking "What is the self?" and what must it "look like" in order to be experienced, or to be the subject of our experience? The self has often been viewed as a specific "thing." Stones are things; the table on which my laptop sits is a thing. And in the same way the table makes it possible for the laptop to sit on it, the structure of the self may make experience and consciousness possible. There must be somebody there, a subject or self who experiences the contents in consciousness. Otherwise, in the absence of such a self or subject, experience would remain impossible. How can there be experience if there is nobody doing the experiencing? Put in a nutshell, there can be no consciousness or experience without a self or subject who can experience and be conscious. Metaphorically speaking, experience and consciousness are the walls that can be erected only on the basis of the ground, the self. But upon what ground does the self stand? It's not just another piece of furniture. The self seems to be part of the floor, a beautifully tiled floor whose patterns shape our perception of the entire room. So is this pattern lost in John and Lucie? Have they lost their sense of self along with their consciousness? We cannot really know the answer to this, but we can explore the question and refine our thinking about it based on findings from neuroscience. To begin this exploration, it is useful to consider what philosophers have said about the self over the centuries.

Is the self a thing? Is it a mental substance, as René Descartes believed? Or is it an illusion? A substance is a specific entity or material that serves as a basis for something else— in this case a self. For instance, the body can be considered a physical substance, whereas the self can be associated with a mental substance. But does the self really exist or is it just a matter of perception—more specifically, an illusion we perceive as real? The question of what exists and is real is a metaphysical question. Earlier philosophers, such as Descartes, assumed that the self exists and is real. This view contrasts with contemporary philosophers. Some of them, such as Dan Zahavi (2005), assume that the self consists of experience or consciousness; it is phenomenal, but it cannot be conceived as a specific mental substance or property. Others such as Merleau-Ponty (1945/1962) and Gallagher (2005) point out the central role of the body in constituting the self. Finally, as we will see below, some philosophers such as Metzinger (2004) are as radical as to deny the existence of a self altogether and consider it as mere illusion. How can we decide which notion of self holds and is compatible with the way the brain works? In order to begin this exploration, let's briefly return to Descartes and his reasons for characterizing the self as mental substance.

Descartes assumed that the self is different from the body: self and body coexist but differ in their fundamental natures: The self is mental whereas the body is physical. The Scottish philosopher David Hume (1748/1777) later questioned this characterization of the self, arguing that there is no self as a mental entity, only a complex set or "bundle" of perceptions of interrelated events that reflect the world in its entirety: In short, there is nothing but the events we perceive. Everything else, such as the assumption of a self as mental entity, is an illusion. The self as mental entity or substance does not exist and is therefore not real.

It's popular in our current culture to side with Hume over Descartes—to reject the idea of self as mental substance and regard it as mere illusion. One major proponent of this view is the German philosopher Thomas Metzinger (Metzinger, 2004). He argues that through our experience, we develop models of the self, so-called *self-models*. These self-models are nothing more than information processes in the brain.

However, since we do not have direct access to these neuronal processes (e.g., all those processes and activities of the cells and neurons in the brain), we tend to assume the presence of an entity that must underlie our own self-models. This entity is then characterized as the self.

According to Metzinger, the assumption of the self as a mental entity results from an erroneous inference from our experience. We cannot experience the neuronal processes in our brain as such. Nobody has ever experienced his or her own brain and its neuronal processes. Because of this lack of direct experience, we cannot trace the outcome of the brain's neuronal processes—the self—back to its original basis—the brain—in our experience. So from where does the sense of self come? Metzinger says that we assume, in our illusory states, that this sense of self must originate in a special entity or substance that is different from the brain. Thus we conclude that the mind and the self are mental entities rather than physical, neuronal entities originating in the brain. Metzinger (2004) argues that the self as a mental entity simply does not exist. Hence, the title of his book: *Being No One*.

Imagine you knock on the door of somebody's house. You knock numerous times, louder with each rap. Finally, you realize that nobody is home; the house is empty. That is the way these philosophers conceive the self. We knock on the door of the body and brain. We can only observe physical activity and, more specifically, neural activity. No mental features are observable at all, let alone a mental "self." In Metzinger's conception, there is simply nobody at home in the brain or body. We are all self-less.

Is there really no one, no *self*? Were Lucie and John "no ones" before the accident, while they were still conscious and riding through the hills, with every memory and feeling that brought them there? We will see that the brain itself says something different. "Yes," we might imagine the brain saying, "There is no mental substance separate and distinct from me, the brain. But that does not mean that I do not construct something that you, as philosopher or neuroscientist, might want to call self."

What is the self? The self is the person or subject that experiences consciousness. It is me, as the subject or self, who experiences the chair on which I sit and the computer on my desk. It is my self or subject who feels pain when I am hurt; others can see my behavior, such as my grimacing face, but do not feel my pain. The self cannot be observed from the outside, in third-person perspective; it can only be experienced from inside, in first-person perspective. For instance, no one has ever observed a self in the brain as object when observing its neural activity from the outside. In contrast, the very same neuroscientists who observe this neural activity in other people's brains experience a self that is doing this observing. Hence the self is a subject rather than an object, one that is closely tied to experience and therefore private and individual.

How Can We Investigate the Self?

How can we get a grip on the self? How can we capture its existence? This question sounds banal, yet it presents us with a paradox. We can observe neural activity in the brain from the outside, in third-person perspective. The self, though, cannot be observed from the outside, only experienced from the inside, in first-person perspective. Since the self cannot be observed in third-person perspective, it cannot be investigated scientifically, and therefore remains a matter for philosophers. However, clever scientists have found a way around this limitation.

To investigate the self experimentally, we need some quantifiable and objective measures that can be observed from a third-person perspective. How can we obtain such measures? Psychologists focusing on memory have observed that items related to ourselves are better remembered than those unrelated (see Northoff et al., 2006). For example, as a resident of Ottawa, Canada, I recall the recent thunderstorm that destroyed several houses in the city much better than a person who, perhaps living in Germany, just heard about it in the news.

Items and stimuli related to oneself claim a superior place in memory. This phenomenon is described as the self-reference effect (SRE). The SRE has been validated in several psychological studies (for an overview, see Klein, 2012; Klein & Gangi, 2010; Northoff, 2014d). Most interestingly, it has been shown to operate in different domains: not only in respect to memory, but also in relation to emotions, sensorimotor functions, faces, words, and so on. In all these different domains, stimuli related to oneself, known as *self-specific stimuli*, are recalled much better than those that are unrelated to oneself, known as *non-self-specific stimuli*, as mentioned previously.

How is the SRE possible? Numerous investigations (for summaries, see Klein, 2012; Klein & Gangi, 2010) show that the SRE is related to different psychological functions ranging from personal memories—including autobiographical memories over memories of facts, or semantic memories—to those cognitive capacities that allow for self-reflection and self-representation. The SRE is not a unitary function, but rather a complex, multifaceted psychological composite of functions and processes.

How Can We Investigate the Self in the Brain?

How can we link the SRE to the brain? Before the introduction of functional imaging techniques such as fMRI at the beginning of the 1990s, most studies focused on the effect of dysfunction or lesions in specific brain regions caused by brain tumours or stroke, for instance. These investigations (Klein, 2012; Klein & Gangi, 2010) revealed that lesions in medial temporal regions that are central to memory recall, such as the hippocampus, change and ultimately abolish the SRE effect. Someone with a lesion in the hippocampus may, for instance, lose all autobiographical memories. Imagine you cannot recall that you were outside in the snowstorm yesterday, amid minus-10-degree temperatures. If you cannot recall it, it is as if it simply did not happen. Your first kiss and your first love, so important until the event of the stroke, all forgotten and gone. No first love, no first kiss. How would you feel? You would say that you lost the history of yourself, your autobiographical memory. That is exactly what happens to patients who suffer a stroke in the hippocampus.

The introduction of brain imaging techniques such as fMRI made these investigations easier. Now we can compare self- and non-self-specific stimuli in the scanner and investigate the underlying brain regions that respond. The basic premise here is that if self-specific stimuli are recalled better than non-self-specific stimuli, they must be processed by the brain in a different way. This difference might be due to higher degrees of neural activity or to activity in different regions.

Using numerous experimental designs, several investigators (for an overview, see Northoff et al., 2006) tested for SRE in the fMRI scanner. For example, subjects were presented trait adjectives related to themselves (e.g., for me, my hometown of Ottawa) and others that were not (Sydney, a city I've never visited). In other tests, the participant was presented with images of his or her own face and the faces of other people. Autobiographical events from the subject's past were also compared with other people's memories. For instance, the picture of your experience of a minus-40-degree snowstorm might be contrasted with a picture of plus-104-degree sunshine on a tropical beach where you have never been. The same goes for faces or names. For example, we could compare your face or name with the face or name of another person and see which parts of the brain these stimuli activate. We presented most of the stimuli either visually or auditorily, and their presentation was usually accompanied by an online judgment about whether or not the stimuli are related and personally meaningful to the research subject.

Self and Subjectivity Go Midline

What did we learn from these studies? And how can we relate the various philosophical concepts of the self to the neuroscientific findings of self-reference? Above, we discussed how psychology, and later neuroscience, quantified the self in terms of the SRE, which describes the different impact of self-referential and non-self-referential stimuli on psychological (e.g., reaction time, recall) and neural (e.g., degree of activity, regions activated) measures. Now we want to briefly highlight some of the findings of recent imaging studies on the SRE.

Two different kinds of regions showed up in the studies using fMRI (for an overview, see Northoff et al., 2006). First, the brain regions specifically activated to process certain domains of human experience, such as emotions and faces, were recruited. For instance, there is a region in the back of the brain, the *fusiform face area*, which specifically processes faces. This region is obviously active during the presentation of faces, no matter whether it is one's own face or another person's face. Importantly, there were no clear differences between self- and non-self-specific stimuli in these domain-specific regions in most studies (e.g., see Northoff et al., 2006)—seeing one's own face did not lead to more activity in the region than observing a stranger's.

There are other brain regions that are not specific to particular domains (also known as *domain-independent regions*) that are involved in the neural processing of self-specific stimuli. Meta-analyses of the various studies demonstrated the involvement of a particular group of regions in the middle of the brain: specifically, the perigenual anterior cingulate cortex (PACC), the ventromedial prefrontal cortex (VMPFC), the dorsomedial prefrontal cortex (DMPFC), the supragenual anterior cingulate cortex (SACC), the posterior cingulate cortex (PCC), and the precuneus. Since they are all located in the midline of the brain, they have been termed *cortical midline structures* (CMS).

The exact role of the midline regions, the CMS, remains unclear. What is clear is that they show some peculiar physiological features, such as extremely high levels of metabolism, resting-state activity, and variability when compared to other regions. Various studies (e.g., Northoff et al., 2006, 2010) also have demonstrated that they are implicated in mental features such as SRE, random thoughts, mind wan-

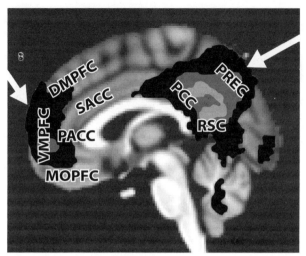

Note. **MOPFC** = medial orbital prefrontal cortex; **PACC** = perigenual anterior cingulate cortex; **VMPFC, DMPFC** = ventro- and dorsomedial prefrontal cortex; **SACC** = supragenual anterior cingulate cortex; **PCC** = posterior cingulate cortex; **PREC** = precuneus; **RSC** = retrosplenial cortex

Figure 3.1 _____

dering, and consciousness. How and why the specific physiological features of the CMS are transformed into mental features remain unclear.

One finding that is consistent throughout the literature is that the CMS are central in distinguishing self-specific or personally relevant stimuli from those that are non-self-specific or not personally relevant. For instance, your own name is a self-specific stimulus, whereas another unknown person's name (if it does not happen to be the same name as yours) is not self-specific for you. How about personally relevant stimuli? If you happen to live in Ottawa, Canada, pictures with snowstorms, blue skies, and a sign of minus-

40-degree temperature are highly relevant to you. Why? Because you have to survive the rather harsh winter in that location. That very same picture is no longer personally relevant to you, though, if you happen to move to Taipei in Taiwan. The Nordic climate of Ottawa is here replaced by a subtropical (I assume) one where snow, let alone snow-storms and minus-40-degree temperatures, are highly unlikely to occur. In that case a picture with palm trees, plus-104-degree temperatures, and a typhoon may be more personally relevant to you.

The Tango of Subjectivity

Why are the CMS and their distinction between self- and non-self-related stimuli so important? The CMS are often regarded as the site of the subject, the self, which experiences consciousness and makes possible its subjective character. We recall from the previous chapter that consciousness is intrinsically subjective, as characterized by a subjective addition of the "what it is like" quality—in our earlier example, the degree of bitterness in the seemingly objective processing of the chocolate. The CMS have been assumed to provide this subjective addition to the otherwise purely objective processing because of their association with self-specificity. And it is this subjective addition that is assumed to make experience, and hence consciousness, possible. In a nutshell, the CMS are assumed to be the site of the self or the subject.

The CMS open novel doors. Being central in processing self-specificity, they open the door to a neuroscience of subjectivity or self. This is most remarkable given that histori-cally, the topic of subjectivity or self was banned from any science, including neuroscience: Science was supposed to address objectively observable contents, not a nonobservable subjective self. The investigation of CMS opens a new door here by allowing for objective investigation of subjectivity itself. That in turn may shed a novel light on an old problem that has plagued past (e.g., Descartes, Kant, and Hume) and present (e.g., Metzinger and Nagel) Western philosophers for centuries: the question of the nature of subjectivity or self.

Can the CMS and the neuroscience of subjectivity resolve this dispute? The CMS allow for distinguishing self- and non-self-specific stimuli—which, if extrapolated, may provide the foundation for a basic understanding of subjectivity. The brain itself and especially its CMS may be essentially subjective in their neural organisation. To deny subjectivity or self and to declare it a mere illusion would consequently amount to neglect and, ultimately, to a rejection of the brain and its CMS. Any denial of subjectivity or self would go against the data and acts of the brain and henceforth be neurally, empirically implausible. Even if we currently do not understand the exact mechanisms by which the seemingly objective neural activity of the CMS is transformed into the subjective features of a self, we cannot deny their role in distinguishing self- and non-self-relatedness. And what empirically is called *self-relatedness* amounts to what philosophically is described as *subjectivity* or *self*. This line of research makes it clear that a neuroscience of subjectivity can shed novel light on, and ultimately resolve, an original philosophical problem—the question of subjectivity or self. Conversely, the philosophy of subjectivity may provide the conceptual apparatus to properly frame the empirical results and to point out their significance for mental features in general. Accordingly, neuroscience and philosophy may want to go hand in hand in order to dance the tango of subjectivity.

The Self Goes Social

"No man is an island," so the saying goes. The self is not isolated. Each of us is in constant contact with other persons, other selves, who provide a reference for us and for our senses of self. Our parents are usually the first to influence our behavioral standards as reference models to which we adapt and whom we aim to follow in childhood. Later, in the often-turbulent years of adolescence, we try to develop a separate self by distinguishing it from our parents' selves. Finally, in adulthood, we may have a spouse, partner, or close friends, on the basis of whom we stabilize and maintain our sense of self in the wake of various changes in our lives. This is to say that the self is very social, and in fact may be deeply social in its very core nature.

How can we investigate the social nature of the self? Various studies have been conducted to investigate different kinds of interactions between different domains such as self, other–social, and rest. Schilbach et al. conducted a meta-analysis that included imaging studies from all three domains of investigation: emotional, resting state, and social–cognitive (Schilbach et al., 2008, 2012). The first step was to analyze the regions implicated in each of the three tasks. This analysis indicated significant neural activity, especially in the midline regions, associated with higher self-specific activity in the spatial fMRI studies. Neural activity in the temporal–parietal junction and the middle temporal gyrus was also observed. These are regions

whose activity has been associated specifically with infer-
ring and understanding other people's thoughts and perspectives. Hence, this study shows that regions such as the
CMS, which are related to the self, are linked with regions
(temporal–parietal junction and the temporal gyrus) that
connect the self to other selves.

In a second step, Schilbach et al. (2012) overlaid the three
tasks—emotional, social–cognitive, and resting state—
in order to detect common underlying areas. This indeed
revealed that the midline regions—the dorsomedial prefrontal cortex and the posterior cingulate cortex—all showed
emotional, social–cognitive tasks, and resting-state activity.
This seems to be rather puzzling. Aren't the midline regions
specific for the self—the individual self as distinguished
from other selves? These and other results seem to contradict that earlier finding. The midline regions are involved in
self-related processing, but they seem to do so in the social
context, in relation to other selves. The self and its self-relatedness seem to be constructed in relation to other selves
and therefore in distinction or difference. The CMS seem to
ask the following question: "How does the individual person
of whose brain I am part of distinguish itself from other persons in its social environment?" The self and its underlying
self-related processing in the CMS seem to be based on the
self's relation to the environment and to other selves.

This finding has radical consequences. In neuroscientific terms it means that *the brain and especially the
CMS are intrinsically social.* There is simply no sharp or
all-or-nothing distinction between the neural level and the
social level. The neural activity in the brain is not inside
the brain and hence nonsocial as distinguished from the
outside with its social environment. The neural activity

itself is social; there is no longer any sharp distinction between neural and social levels; the brain and its CMS are intrinsically, or by default, *neurosocial*. Neural or social? That is simply a fallacious dichotomy. The brain and especially the CMS and their involvement in the experience of self teach us better that such dichotomy is an illusion. The notion of an isolated self, a nonsocial self, somewhere deep inside the brain or a mind is indeed an illusion. Metzinger is right here. But the notion of a social or *neurosocial* self is not an illusion. It is real—real in our experience and real in our brain and its CMS.

Neural Overlap between Rest and Self

We have seen that the midline regions, the CMS, are central in generating subjectivity or sense of self. How do they do it? One may assume that cognitive, affective, and sensorimotor functions generate subjectivity or self. Various investigators assume that the self originates from the meta-representation of the brain's neural activity: The neural activity related to more basic functions such as sensory functions is processed (or better, reprocessed) a second time in another set of regions, like the sensory cortical activity may be reprocessed in the midline regions, with such reprocessing leading to a sense of self. The brain is hereby meta-represented and may thereby be identified as a cognitive self, as Damasio (2010) and Churchland (2002) assume. Alternatively, one may assume the self via the neural activity elicited by the body and its vegetative and sensorimotor functions. The self is then determined in a vegetative–affective or sensorimotor way, as Christoff, Cosmelli, Legrand, and Thompson (2011) and Panksepp (1998 b) assume.

Are these accounts of the self in terms of cognitive, affective, or sensorimotor functions plausible? Sure, they concern aspects of the self. The self is manifest in our cognitions, emotions, perceptions, and actions; we simply cannot avoid this self, and we carry it around with us all the time. But that seems to confuse the issue of the manifestation and origin of self: The self is *manifest* in sensorimotor, affective, and cognitive functions, but it may not *originate* in these functions and their respective neural correlates. Instead, self or subjectivity may originate in something deeper, something that is more basic and underlies all these functions. This possibility leads us back to the spontaneous or intrinsic activity of the resting state of the brain, which remains independent of any extrinsic stimulus-induced activity and its various sensorimotor, cognitive, and affective properties.

How are self and rest related to each other? Various investigators have demonstrated neural overlap between self-related processing and resting-state activity levels in that the former did not elicit changes in the latter. Self-specific stimuli such as your name do not change the level of neural activity in the anterior midline regions of PACC and VMPFC when compared to their resting state. There is simply no activity change in these regions when processing self-specific stimuli. This finding has been shown in various imaging studies by ourselves and others (d'Argembeau et al., 2005; Schneider et al., 2008). We therefore speak of a rest–self overlap to convey the correspondence in neural activity levels during resting-state and self-specific neural activity.

The finding of neural overlap between resting-state and self-related activity is really puzzling. You would expect that self-specific stimuli, as the most important stimuli for you, would elicit the highest degree of activity change in the brain, specifically in the CMS. High relevance = high-activity change. You would think that the brain encodes high-personal-relevance items in commensurately high-activity changes so that the self-specific stimuli stand out when compared to non-self-specific ones and to the rest of the brain. That is the way you experience your *self*: You stand out in the environment when compared to others. You would consequently expect your brain to do the same, to make the self stand out with high-activity changes.

That high-activity change, though, does not seem to be the case. Rather, the opposite holds. Your self—the basic subjectivity of your experience and consciousness—does not seem to stand out at all; it rather overlaps with your brain's ongoing resting-state activity. Your brain's resting-state activity seems to already contain some information about your self, a basic trace of subjectivity. And suddenly the findings of rest–self overlap seem to make sense. In the same way the resting-state activity of your brain is continuously present, active and changing, your own self is continuously present and changing. "Aha! That is why I cannot avoid my own self," you might say now. "I always carry it with me no matter where I go and how often I switch continents. To leave my self behind would mean to leave my brain and its resting state behind— which remains impossible since then I would be dead—brain-dead."

Subjectivity in Rest

The rest–self overlap does not only open novel doors but also turns around the whole building. What was long considered the pinnacle of the mind—self and subjectivity—seems now to be located at its very bottom: in the resting-state activity of the brain. Instead of looking toward the lofty heights of the upper floors when searching for a mind, we may need to look downward to the basement of the building, the brain's resting-state activity. Self or subjectivity is an intrinsic ingredient of the brain itself and its intrinsic activity. Brain and intrinsic activity are, by default, subjective and cannot avoid constructing some kind of self. This is a radical thesis that reverberates deeply into neuroscience and its view of the seemingly purely objective brain, as well as into philosophy and its view of subjectivity as the province of higher mental features.

Because the rest–self overlap has such major implications, it is essential to ground it empirically as solidly as possible. One way to do that is to investigate it on the cellular level: whether, for instance, the firing rates of single neurons in the PACC do or do not change in response to the subject's name. If there is a rest–self overlap, one would not expect the firing rates to change during the subject's processing of his or her own name, whereas if the self is supposed to stand out neurally, one would expect the firing rate of the cells to increase. Most interestingly, we (Lipsman et al., 2014) indeed observed that the presentation of the subject's own name did not change the cells' firing rate in the PACC (rather than, as expected, inducing major changes in firing rates).

These findings suggest that the spontaneous or resting-state firing rates somehow recognize the person's own name as a well-known stimulus and therefore "decide that they do not need to change their firing rates." If you already know the person in front of you very well, you do not need to change your behavior and become formal. If, in contrast, you do not know the person, you will certainly change your behavior and become more formal. The cells in the PACC seem to "think the same": "Why change my firing rates if I already know the stimulus, 'my' own name?"

How is it possible that the resting state "knows" the self and its name? The only way for that to be possible is that the PACC, in its resting-state or spontaneous activity patterns, must already contain some information about the self. Because we characterized the resting-state activity in previous chapters by a spatial–temporal structure, we can now assume that the information about the self is encoded into that spatial–temporal structure. Is the self encoded in specific spatial or temporal patterns of neural activity? For example, the self may be encoded in particular frequency ranges in the brain's fluctuations. In the moment the resting state is altered, the self is changed too. Self and resting state are intrinsically related to each other. Without self, the resting state no longer has any spatial–temporal structure, and without the resting state, no self can be constructed. In short: There is no self without rest and no rest without self.

The Relational Self

The self is encoded in the resting-state activity of the brain and its spatial–temporal structure. What, though, do we mean by the concepts of *structure* and *organization* with respect to the self? The structure must be virtual and spatial–temporal in that it spans the physical boundaries of the brain, the body, and the environment. Does this mean that we have to revert to a mental structure and organization that are distinct from the physical structure and organization of the brain? No! The results from neuroscience clearly link the self with neuronal processes related to both intra-individual and interindividual experiences—for example, social interaction. There is thus a neuronal basis for the distinct aspects of the self within the context of the brain, the body, and the environment.

Let's further explain this relation between brain, body, and environment. On the one hand, the self can be viewed as intrinsically linked to the body—the *embodied self*. On the other hand, because it is based on self-reference, the self can also be viewed as intrinsically linked to the environment— the *embedded* and *social self*, as suggested by the advocates of the concept of a social self. Consequently, the self cannot be regarded as an entity located somewhere in the brain, isolated from both body and environment. The brain's neural activity is intrinsically *neurosocial*: The brain cannot avoid the social–environmental context when encoding stimuli in its intrinsic activity. To state this point another way: The brain's intrinsic activity is neurosocial, rather than merely neuronal, and it may construct a virtual spatial–temporal structure spanning the brain, body, and environment, making it a *virtual, social, spatial–temporal* structure that we investigators like to call the *self*. As we have seen, this statement is empirically supported by the neural overlap between resting-state activity and self-related activity.

Why is the characterization of the self as virtual, social, and spatial–temporal relevant? Recall John and Lucie. The activity in their brains is no longer neurosocial; it is merely neural, without the social component. This is why they and their brains are disconnected from their bodies and the environment, ultimately culminating in their loss of spatial–temporal experience: the loss of consciousness.

What does this intrinsically embodied and social nature imply for the conceptual characterization of the self? The self may be described as a spatial–temporal structure and organization rather than an entity—be it mental or physical. Such a structure and organization develops throughout childhood and adolescence, with changes taking place even in adulthood. Despite all these changes, for most of us there is also persistence and continuity across time, which then accounts for what can be described as *identity* or *self-continuity*. An exploratory study (Ersner-Hershfield, Wimmer, Knutson et al., 2009) has associated this attribute of identity or self-continuity with the midline structures of the brain (discussed in detail in Chapter 7).

Note that *no assumption of mind* is needed here to explain the phenomenon of self. Only the brain and the relation it constructs to body and environment on the basis of its neurosocial activity are required. Metzinger (2004) and others who assume that the self is nonexistent are correct in the sense that there is no mind at home. However, they are wrong in their inference that the self does not exist. No, it does not exist as mind, as a separate mental entity. Nor does it exist as a purely neural or physical entity, since it cannot be found in brain, body, or environment per se. It can be found, though, in the *relationship* between brain, body, and environment. *The self is a relation rather than an entity*; it is intrinsically relational, a continuous process of structuring and organizing the relation between brain, body, and environment. This conceptualization provides a novel philosophical approach to explain the self as a relational and process-based self rather than a mind- or entity-based concept of self.

In addition to its philosophical relevance, the characterization of the self as the product of the social, virtual, and spatial–temporal organization of the brain's intrinsic activity harbors important clinical implications. Lucie's and John's brains no longer connect them to their respective social environments in a virtual and spatial–temporal way, so they no longer show any active behavior toward the environment. One could say that the self of each of them, as defined in this sense, remains absent. However, they were lucky: The cortical midline structures of their brains "came back" in relation to their bodies and environments, as manifested in their reawakening—regaining consciousness— after 3 months.

Chapter 4

DEPRESSION AND THE MIND–BRAIN PROBLEM

═══════════ PREVIEW ═══════════

Are psychiatric diseases actually disorders of the resting state rather than of the mind?

Psychiatric disorders are often considered the last barrier of neuroscience. Neuroscientists have actively investigated the neural bases of various cognitive functions, such as attention and memory, which in earlier times were associated with the mind. Even more recently, neuroscientists have begun to reveal the neural mechanisms underlying mental features such as self and consciousness, as we have seen in the previous chapters. However, although the neural components of many neurological disorders such as epilepsy, Parkinson's disease, and the dementia of Alzheimer's disease have been located, the neural bases and origins of psychiatric disorders remain unclear. Despite all our knowledge of their biochemical and molecular underpinnings (see below), psychiatric disorders continue to be considered disorders of the mind: *mental* disorders (for instance, as described in the "bible" of psychiatric diagnosis that still uses this descriptor in its latest edition: *The Diagnostic and Statistical Manual of Mental Disorders*).

In this chapter I show that to understand depression, for example, we need to view the brain and its resting state in a more complex way by considering its genetic, environmental, and temporal contexts. This new perspective sheds new light on our view of the brain in general and especially in regard to the old philosophical conundrum of the relationship between mind and brain. Let's begin with a purely fictive case example that shows some of the typical features of depression, as individuals experience it in daily life.

CASE EXAMPLE

Judy is a 41-year-old woman, a high-profile policy adviser working at a major foreign policy think tank in Washington, DC. Only 2 weeks ago, Judy was on top of the world after receiving the long desired promotion to her dream position. One week later, however, Judy's happiness and lightness disappeared. To the surprise of her colleagues, she showed up at work looking gloomy and tired. Though her new position did not begin for 3 more weeks, she already felt its burden and load. She lay in bed for hours before falling asleep and then woke up early, before 5 A.M., restless, her mind racing with doubts: Was she really capable of fulfilling the new position? Was she the person to devise a new American foreign policy for Russia?

Her mood continued to deteriorate, growing darker, gloomier. Soon all her enthusiasm about the promotion was gone, replaced with anxiety and dread. Known around the office as outgoing and sociable, Judy surprised her colleagues by withdrawing into her office and no longer talking to the people around her. She felt isolated and unable to communicate with them, and as she became more and more convinced that she was the wrong person for the position, she felt guilty about the promotion. "It must have all been a mistake," she started saying to herself. She considered resigning before even starting in the new role. Her sleep continued to deteriorate. Even the 4 or 5 hours she used to get became impossible. She would just lie in her bed, quite awake, with circulating, ruminating thoughts. Her outlook was especially gloomy in the morning. The only periods of relative lightness she experienced occurred in the evening.

Eventually Judy couldn't even manage to get out of bed in the morning. What was the point of breakfast, which required so much concentration and effort, when she wasn't hungry anyway? Her whole body began to ache and her heart felt like it was pounding at an unnatural rate.

Worst of all, Judy stopped feeling any connection to her husband and her two children, who were 10 and 12 years old. She felt as though they were not her own and that they deserved a much better mother, a much better wife. Her husband knew what was happening. He had lived through two previous episodes with her, each related to originally positive events. Both times she had shown more or less the same symptoms: The episode began with sleeplessness, doubt, guilt, and loss of appetite; then she disconnected from him and the children, and from her social environment. "The depression locks her up," he would tell friends and family. He also knew what came next: She would develop suicidal thoughts, even if she were too embarrassed to admit it.

Judy's side of the family knew the depressive condition well. Her grandmother, who had escaped the Russian Revolution by fleeing to America, and her aunt had both suffered from the same symptoms on occasion, though it was unclear whether they had ever received psychiatric treatment. For Judy, at this point of her descent, admission to the hospital became inevitable.

The Gene–Brain Problem

What is depression? Judy's case example does not describe the usual depression (or major depressive disorder/MDD, as it is called by psychiatrists) we refer to when we say, "I'm depressed." Judy's symptoms point to a severe depression, a clinically relevant depression that incapacitates her. Thoughts, perceptions, actions, emotions—they all become frozen, immobile, and negative. "You are in a dark hole without exit or any ray of sun," a patient told me. "How does it feel? Terrible, anxious, and desperate—that is exactly how I feel in depression."

Depression has a long human history. Many artists have written about it, painted it, even sculpted it. In earlier times, particularly medieval times, depression was thought to be related to an abnormal darkness of the soul, an absence or departure of the life spirits. This legacy has led to much stigma, and people with depression were often castigated. Now we seem to know better, though there is still a stigma attached to having any kind of "mental disorder." As we will see, depression is related to the brain, which has been known for the past 40 years or so; however, what is novel is that depression may be traced to alterations in its own intrinsic activity and the latter's relation to the environment.

There are two typical components underlying depression. The first is the genetic component, as documented in Judy's family history. This genetic component in depression is clear, but the exact genetic pathways are not: We don't yet know why, how, or when the experience-dependent expression of genes is transferred and carries a risk or depression for the subsequent generation. We also aren't sure how the genes impact neural activity in the brain.

There is one particular biochemical substance in the brain, serotonin, which seems to be prominent in depression. Serotonin originates in subcortical brain regions, particularly a region called the *raphe nucleus*. This nucleus sends serotonin to the rest of the brain and especially the upper parts, the frontal, temporal, and parietal cortices, so that serotonin can modulate the cortex's level of neural activity. The SSRIs (selective serotonin reuptake inhibitors), such as the famous antidepressant Prozac, can be used for therapy of depressive symptoms. Because Prozac is known to modulate serotonin, its efficacy in alleviating symptoms of depression permit the assumption that changes in the level of serotonin are central to depression.

For example, the impact of certain genes that modulate production of the serotonin levels and affect its transport have been investigated on both biochemical and behavioral levels, as well as in neuropsychiatric disorders such as depression, where serotonin seems to play a central role. These investigations have shown that each of the relevant genes may be present in different variants, which would entail slightly different expressions of substances such as serotonin (for a review, see Northoff, 2013). *Polymorphism* is the term used to refer to different constellations of underlying genes. For instance, one and the same genes may be present in two different serotonin-related gene variants (where one and the same genes can occur in different forms or variants, called *alleles*). Particular constellations of these polymorphisms may be risk factors for disorders such as depression if certain variants predominate over others. Recent investigations (see Northoff, 2013) have demonstrated that patients with depression have a higher incidence of certain polymorphism coding for a specific substance that transports serotonin, called *promoter polymorphism* (*5-HTTLPR*) of the serotonin transporter gene (*SLC6A4*), when compared to nondepressed patients.

This particular polymorphism also impacts neural activity. Imaging studies have shown that in healthy individuals, those with the genetic variant called the *S-allele* show increased neural activity in the amygdala, a region specifically involved in processing emotions. This is not the case in individuals carrying another genetic variant, the *L-allele*. It could be that the genes *S- or L-alleles* that they inherit (and more specifically, particular polymorphisms) put these individuals at risk for increased amygdala activity and consequently for depression. Due to her genes and their polymorphisms, for instance, Judy's amygdala may be predisposed to react abnormally to life events, such as taking on the new position. Her amygdala response, in turn, sets the whole cycle of subsequent neural and psychological events into motion. Hence it is a genetic–neural predisposition—the genes predisposing the amygdala to react abnormally to life events— that may be a central risk factor for depression. However, the exact mechanisms of how these genetic–neural linkages occur and the kind of predispositions they exert on the brain and its neural–mental transformation remain unclear.

The research on depression carries an important philosophical implication for untangling the mind–brain problem. Contemporary philosophers often equate mind and brain, and argue that the mind is nothing but the brain; mental features are conceived as neural features. However, the depression research shows that mental features cannot be reduced solely to neural features—the mind is *not* just the brain and its neural activity. The mind and its mental features are the products of the brain plus genes; the search for the mechanisms underlying neural–mental transformation need to be complemented by the one for genetic–neural linkages. If we want to understand the brain's neural features and how they transform into mental features, we need to understand the genetic component of the brain and how it links to neural features. One may consequently speak of a gene–brain problem that complements, if not replaces, the mind–brain problem, as is discussed in the next section.

The World–Brain Problem

There is more to the genome than polymorphisms. Initially it was thought that genes directly control the level of specific substances such as serotonin. That is not the case. In addition to the polymorphisms, it is clear that there are multiple copies of the same gene, called *copy number variants* (CNV). However, as in real life, the copying process may not always go smoothly, so that there may be defects hidden in the various copies of the same gene. The different defects—whether deletions, insertions, or duplications—may be particularly relevant in psychiatric disorders such as schizophrenia and depression. We don't know exactly what happens in these cases; the genome is far from being understood at this point in time.

These copying processes can be altered and disrupted by severely stressful life events, such as experiencing bombing during war, and early traumatic life events, such as maltreatment or sexual abuse. Such harsh stressors leave traces in the genome in ways that are still unclear. The effects could manifest in an abnormally high number of defects in the CNV, as described above. Whether such abnormal copying can account for the strong impact of life events in triggering depression, as in Judy's case, also remains unclear. What we can say, however, is that the genome is tightly interwoven with the environment, to the point that the latter can exert direct impact on the former. The experts term this mutual influence the *gene × environment interaction*. We will see that this close interrelationship with the environment also holds true for the brain itself. Here, we could speak of the *brain × environment* interaction (see Northoff, 2013).

Why is all of this relevant for our larger philosophical view of the brain and its relationship to what philosophers call *mind*? Because it tells us that genes are not simply genes and that the brain is not just the brain. I've already demonstrated that the brain is not only neural activity but that it is also regulated by genes and their genetic–neural linkages. And the genes are not just the genes. We already saw the complex variables that polymorphisms and CNVs add to the total picture, and we are just beginning to understand and unravel that intricacy. Factors we cannot even think of at this point in time will no doubt be revealed in the future. The most salient point here is that genes are strongly dependent upon their environmental context and the respective life events in terms of how they are expressed. Genes are not just genes; they are genes plus the environment. This basic reality has important impli-cations not only for psychiatric disorders such as depres-sion, but also for characterizing the brain in general. The brain is situated not only in a genetic context but also in an environmental or ecological context. One could postulate that it is exactly its neural–genetic and neural–ecological character that allows the brain's neural activity to be transformed into what we experience as mental activity. Put more technically, the brain's neural–mental transformations are based on its genetic–neural linkages and its ecological or environmental integration.

This formulation has important implications for the philosopher and his or her view of the mind–brain problem. The mind cannot be simplistically reduced to the brain and its neural activity. The brain itself is brain *plus* genes *plus* environment. Maybe then the philosopher wants to reverse this view. Rather than questioning the nature of mind and how it relates to the brain, he or she may want to question the nature of the brain and how it relates to genes and ultimately to the world. The original mind–brain problem is then replaced by what can be called the *gene–brain* problem and, even more important, the world–brain problem. The answer to both problems may carry the solution for the nature of mental features and how they relate to the brain's neural features: the original mind–brain problem. If so, the philosopher may want to replace the original mind–brain problem with the gene–brain and world–brain problems.

Delayed and Immediate Therapy: Time and the Brain

Another biochemical substance relevant in depression, glutamate, increases neural activity; that is, it produces *excitation*, as the researchers term it. The receptors for chemical substances that act on glutamate modulate its level. One such chemical substance is ketamine. Ketamine seems to block the receptors and thus closes the door, so to speak, for glutamate to enter the room and excite the neurons. In more technical terms, ketamine decreases the abnormally high levels of neural excitation and resting-state activity in depression (Northoff et al., 2011); this action seems to normalize abnormally high levels of arousal and excitation from which these patients suffer on a mental level. Unlike other drugs, ketamine seems to exert a direct and almost immediate therapeutic effect in patients with depression. Why and how patients with deep depression and strong suicidal thoughts react especially well to ketamine is not yet clear.

What is clear is that the therapeutic efficacy of ketamine can be considered a major step forward. The direct and immediate relief that ketamine exerts contrasts with other commonly used antidepressants—mainly drugs that modulate serotonin and other biochemical substances such as adrenaline and noradrenaline—which usually take 10–20 days to show some therapeutic effects. In the meantime, neither the patient nor the psychiatrist can do anything but wait to see if the antidepressant will help. We have no idea which one will work and which one will not work in which patient. This time delay is now shortened by ketamine and its immediate therapeutic effects (though side effects of the drug can induce dizziness and perceptual changes).

What does the distinction between delayed and immediate therapeutic effects tell us about the brain in general? It tells us that we need to consider the temporal dimension when characterizing brain functions. The brain has different neural mechanisms that act on different time scales: short, medium, and long ones. There is a multitude of time scales operating side by side in the brain, with each having probably its own mechanisms and specific effects. We currently do not understand the different time scales with their different mechanisms and variable effects, let alone how they are linked and integrated with each other. It may be the case, for instance, that psychiatric disorders simply result from abnormal integration of the different time scales operating in the brain. This possibility, however, is rather speculative at this point in time from the empirical perspective.

The Time–Brain Problem: Stress and (Lack of) Sleep

Let's return to the second typical feature of depression shown in our example. The onset of a depression episode is often triggered by life events, as in Judy's case. These life events can be negative or positive; they can include loss of a loved one, job problems, job promotions, and so on. Depression is often associated with stress—that is, stress as it is subjectively perceived. Even if an event is not objectively stressful, the person experiencing it may nevertheless perceive it in a negative way. It is the subjective perception that is altered. So although the job promotion had long been Judy's dream, for example, when it finally became true she perceived it in a highly stressful way, worrying about whether she would be able to handle the requirements.

Interestingly, some studies by Gerald Sanacora in New York show that glutamate, the excitatory substance, appears at reduced levels in the visual cortex of patients with depression (e.g., Sanacora, Mason, & Krystal, 2000). This discovery has been complemented by the findings of Golomb et al. (2009), which show psychological abnormalities in visual perception as related to neural abnormalities in the visual cortex. Do these visual abnormalities account for the abnormal perception of stress in life events? We currently do not know, but data indicate that perception, especially visual perception, is altered in depression in that these patients perceive shapes in a more blurred way.

Another typical feature of depression is sleep problems and mood differences between morning and evening. Judy suffered from the typical morning dip in mood. Patients with depression are especially gloomy upon awakening when the perceived load of the whole day is ahead of them. There is some relief in the evening when the load is no longer as heavy, probably because the day is finally over. In neurobiological terms, the brain possesses a circadian rhythm system that regulates the sleep–wake cycle; this circadian system, in a little region in the brain called the *nucleus suprachiasmaticus*, seems to be abnormal in patients with depression. Interestingly, imposed sleep deprivation, whereby people are not allowed to sleep for half a night or the full night, nets some beneficial effects in the person the subsequent day. Why and how? Those questions, too, remain unanswered for now.

These observations further solidify our assumption that the brain operates on different time scales. There are short time scales involving milliseconds and longer ones like the 24-hour circadian time scales. How does the brain integrate all these time scales and their differences? It seems that in depression there is some *dis*coordination between the different time scales, resulting in the symptoms that typify this disorder. These data indicate that the brain is not a purely neural organ; rather, it is a temporal organ, a temporal engine, which produces, constructs, and integrates different times scales.

This temporal element sheds further light on the concept of the brain that is relevant to philosophical formulations.

We cannot consider the brain and its neural activity independent of time. Time and its different time scales are an essential feature of the brain. As said before, the brain is not just the brain. Now we can add another factor to our characterization of the brain. The brain is the brain plus time (plus genes, plus world). This raises the metaphysical question about the relationship between the existence of time in the world and the brain: How is the brain and its neural activity linked to the time in the world and its different time scales? That is, do the different time scales in the world have parallel manifestations in the brain, and how are they integrated and linked with each other? That these time scales are integrated is supported empirically by the adaptation of the brain and its nucleus suprachiasmaticus to the rhythms of day and night. Amazing, isn't it? How can the neural activity of the brain in this region be temporally structured and control the rest of the brain according to the rhythm of the light of day and the darkness of night in the outer world? The brain and its time are apparently closely linked to the time in the world. We may therefore want to speak of a time–brain problem that complements the gene–brain and world–brain problems.

Increased Self-Focus and Body Focus

To recap: Depression is a psychiatric disorder that is characterized by extremely negative emotions, suicidal thoughts, hopelessness, diffuse bodily symptoms, lack of pleasure, ruminations, and enhanced stress sensitivity. The self is also altered in these patients, showing an "increased self-focus" (Northoff, 2007). One author described this self-focus as follows:

She sat by the window, looking inward rather than looking out. Her thoughts were consumed with her sadness.
She viewed her life as a broken one, and yet she could not
place her finger on the exact moment it fell apart. "How
did I get to feel this way?" she repeatedly asked herself.
By asking, she hoped to transcend her depressed state;
through understanding, she hoped to repair it. Instead,
her questions led her deeper and deeper inside herself—further away from the path that would lead to her
recovery (Treynor, Gonzalez, & Nolen-Hoeksema, 2003,
p. 247).

This description of a depressed patient shows three crucial
characteristics: increased self-focus, association of the self
with negative emotions, and increased cognitive processing
of the self. Let us start with increased self-focus. Like Judy,
almost all patients with depression look inward rather than
outward, focusing very much on themselves, no longer able
to readily shift their focus to others. Social psychology theory describes self-focused attention as a focus on contents
that stem from internal sources (e.g., one's body, mind),
rather than from external origin (e.g., the environment).
The self-focus may also involve an enhanced awareness of
one's present or past physical behavior (i.e., heightened cog-
nizance of what one is doing or how one perceives one's own
self with what kinds of qualities in experience—the "what
it is like"). In addition to such increased self-focus, the
depressed patient's focus is often on his or her body, which
results in the subjective perception of diffuse bodily symptoms. The increased self-focus may therefore be accompanied by what I call *increased body focus*.

Why are self-focus and body focus relevant in philosophical terms? They tell us that self and body are closely linked to each other because the increased self-focus is often accompanied by an increased body focus. That association, though, does not mean that we can reduce the self to the body; they are distinct from each other rather than being identical, as philosophers such as K. Christoff and E. Thompson assume, who identify the self with the body (see Christoff et al., 2011). Moreover, it is not only that the self is subjective, but so is the body; it can be experienced in a subjective way, conceptualized as the *lived body* by Merleau-Ponty (1945/1962). It is this subjective or lived body that is altered in depression.

To further clarify: The objective body is the purely physical body that we can observe in others—whether somebody is short or tall, fat or thin. The subjective body, in contrast, refers to the way the respective individual experiences his or her body. One may subjectively experience one's own body as fat, even though objectively it is slim or even dangerously thin (e.g., in cases of anorexia). Thus there must be considerable discrepancy possible between observation of the objective body and the experience of the subjective body.

What exactly is the lived body? The *lived body* is the objective physical body plus the way we subjectively experience that very same body. Contemporary philosophers such as Christoff and Thompson (see Christoff et al., 2011) and Gallagher (2005) have now argued that the body, the lived body, carries the key to the mind–brain problem—which may therefore be conceived as mind–*body* problem. The subjective nature of the lived body makes mental features possible and may therefore be considered the key to understanding how the mind is generated and what it is. Put in a nutshell, *the mind is the lived body*.

That statement, however, confuses effect and origin. The lived body is an *effect* of what philosophers like to call *mind*, rather than its origin. We perceive external and purely objective contents like the table in front of us in a subjective way. Analogously, we also experience purely internal contents such as the objective body in a subjective way, resulting in what is described as the *lived body*. There is thus a subjective addition to the processing of the purely objective content, irrespective of whether it is of internal origin (the body) or external origin (the table).

Where is this subjective addition, which allows us to go beyond the purely objective content in our experience, coming from? I assume that this subjective addition originates in the brain and its resting state. The brain's resting state adds this subjective addition to its own neural processing of the objective internal and external contents. The brain's resting state may thus be the origin of the lived body, as distinguished from the objective body. The lived body is thereby an effect, rather than the origin, of the subjective addition. To now conceive the lived body as the origin of the mind and, even more dramatic, as the solution to the mind–brain problem in general is to simply confuse effects (the lived body) and origin (the resting state of the brain).

Decreased Focus on the Environment and the Mind's Reciprocal Balance

The increased self-focus and body focus imply that the depressed person's attention is no longer directed toward his or her relations to the environment and its events, as in healthy individuals, but rather on him- or herself. The environment shifts into the background. With this *decreased environment focus*, the patient's subjective perception and experience are directed toward his or her body and thoughts, as we've already seen, resulting in increased self-focus. This means that in depression, the person's focus is unilaterally shifted toward the self at the expense of his or her perceptions of, and relations with, the environment.

This perspective is supported by empirical data. Studies that have assessed self-focused attention, using diverse measures and methodologies, all converge on the finding of an increased and perhaps prolonged level of self-focused attention in depression (Ingram, 1990). What remains unclear, though, is whether this increased self-focus is purely explicit and thus conscious, or whether it is present at an implicit and thus unconscious level. If conscious, one would assume that it is related to stimulus-induced or task-evoked activity and the respective cognitive functions. If, in contrast, it remains unconscious, it must be generated at a deeper level—as, for instance, by the brain's resting-state activity. This possibility is explored later in this chapter.

Finally, there is also increased cognitive processing of the self. Referring back to our case example, Judy thinks about herself and her mood and tries desperately to discover the reasons for her depression, but as a result she only sinks deeper and deeper into the depressed mood. This cognitive processing of the self is termed *rumination*. It is often considered to be a method of attempting to cope with negative moods that involves increased self-focused attention and self-reflection.

Taken together, patients with depression suffer from the combination of increased self-focus and body focus with a decreased environment focus. What does this tell us about the brain and its relationship to the mind, the mind–

brain problem? It tells us that the brain needs to be conceived within the triangle of self, body, and environment.
These three (self, body, and environment) seem to stand in
a balance with reciprocal modulation: Increase in self- and
body focus seems to occur at the expense of the environment focus, which is decreased. The converse—increased
environment focus with decrease in self- and body focus—
can be observed in the extreme opposite to depression:
that is, in mania, in which state patients are abnormally
happy and excited.

What does this reciprocal balance imply for our characterization of mind and brain? The reciprocal balance
concerns the balance between different kinds of mental
contents: contents in the mind as related to self, body, or
environment. The mind can therefore be characterized by
a reciprocal balance between different contents within the
triangular relationship between self, body, and environment. Where is this reciprocal balance with the triangular
relationship between self, body, and environment coming
from? It may come from within the mind itself, but that view
would require us to fall back into a traditional philosophical view that assumes some kind of mind entity and then to
raise the question of how that very same mind is related to
the brain. Why not start with the brain itself and its neural
organization of resting-state activity? That is the path I pursue here.

The Brain's Intrinsic Design Features: Midline Structures and Reciprocal Balance

From where does the reciprocal balance that occurs in
the triangular relationship between the self, the body, and

the environment come? To answer this question, I return to brain imaging studies of depression. Overviews (or *meta-analyses*) of all imaging studies investigating human depression that focused on resting-state activity reported hyperactivity in several midline regions in both the pre-frontal cortex and the subcortical areas. In contrast to the midline regions, resting-state activity was hypoactive in the regions at the outer surface, more laterally placed, such as the dorsolateral prefrontal cortex (DLPFC). Aha! Some reciprocal balance here with hyperactive midline regions and hypoactive lateral regions. Is the medial–lateral balance thus reciprocally modulated and related to the reciprocal balance between self- and environment focus and their respective contents?

In addition to the human research, there are models of depression based on animal research that aim to mimic depressive behavior in, for instance, rats and mice. One such model is the forced swim tests. In this test rats or mice are placed into water and are thus forced to swim. The rats or mice that are predisposed for depression will not swim and barely move in their novel water environment, just like the human patients do not move much. Why are such animal models of depression needed? We can study certain molecular mechanisms and genetic effects by modulating target molecules or genes—which we certainly cannot do in this way in humans. For instance, we can study the causal effects of certain genes on the neural activity in a particular region such as the amygdala or the midline regions. The results from those kinds of studies provide the causal underpinnings to the observations we make in human brains. Most interestingly, the modulation of different molecules and genes all leads to abnormal increases in resting-state activity in the medial regions in rat and mice prefrontal cortex (Alcaro, Panksepp, Witczak, Hayes, & Northoff, 2010). This finding suggests that the midline region is apparently the final pathway into which the different molecular and genetic changes converge, thereby eliciting abnormally high resting-state activity.

In sum, there seems to be convergence between human and animal findings, with both showing increased resting-state activity in the medial regions of the brain and rather decreased in the lateral regions. This is important information because it indicates a reciprocal balance between medial and lateral regions and their respective contents as related to self and environment. This reciprocal balance between resting-state activity in medial and lateral regions is apparently disturbed in depression: The resting-state activity seems to be abnormally high in the medial regions, both cortically and subcortically. Meanwhile, resting-state activity is abnormally low in more lateral regions, such as the DLPFC.

How are these resting-state abnormalities related to the increased self-focus and its imbalance with the decreased environment focus in cases of depression? Some recent fMRI studies (Freton et al., 2014; Grimm et al., 2011) presented self-specific stimuli, using either emotional pictures or words (known as *trait adjectives*), to patients with depression. The researchers observed that these patients showed abnormal stimulus-induced activity in response to the self-specific stimuli (when compared to the non-self-specific).

Behaviorally, patients with depression attributed abnormally high degrees of self-specificity to negative emotional stimuli, as compared to healthy individuals. This abnormally high degree of self-specificity, as well as the sever- ity of depression symptoms, correlated with the degree of abnormal activity in the midline regions during the admin- istration of self-specific stimuli. This means that the abnor- mal stimulus-induced activity in midline regions of these patients seems to be closely related to their assignment of abnormal degrees of self-specificity to extrinsic stimuli, as well as to their depressive symptoms.

Before exploring the larger implications, I want to make a cautionary remark. These data do not show the rest- ing-state abnormalities themselves to be related to the increased self-focus. Instead, it is rather the *stimulus-in- duced activity* in response to *extrinsic self-specific stim- uli* that is abnormal in these patients. The direct linkage between resting-state activity and increased self-focus remains to be demonstrated. Furthermore, it remains unclear how, for instance, the lateral cortical resting-state hypoactivity contributes to the decreased environment focus in these patients.

The increased resting-state activity in the midline accounts for the increased self-focus (and possibly the increased body focus too), and the decrease in the lateral region is related to the decreased environment focus. We can thus see how the reciprocal balance between mental con- tents related to self and environment can be traced to the reciprocal balance between medial and lateral resting-state activity levels. The resting state itself and its organization or spatial structure in medial and lateral regions predisposes a reciprocal balance between internal (self- and body related) and external (environmental) mental contents.

This predisposition toward balance carries major philo- sophical implications. No mind is needed to account for the

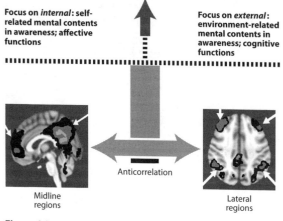

Relational self: *Balance between internal (i.e., self-related) focus and external (i.e., environment-related) focus*

Focus on *internal*: self-related mental contents in awareness; affective functions

Focus on *external*: environment-related mental contents in awareness; cognitive functions

Anticorrelation

Midline regions

Lateral regions

Figure 4.1a

reciprocal balance between the different mental contents. Instead of the mind, we need to understand the spatial (and also temporal) structure of the resting-state activity and how it is related to, and operates in, medial and lateral regions. We currently do not understand the neuronal mechanisms underlying the reciprocal balance between medial and lateral regions. One could also imagine a nonreciprocal balance, in which case an increase in self-focus would be accompanied by an increase (rather than decrease) in environment focus. Apparently the brain shows certain intrinsic design features that predispose it toward a reciprocal rather than nonreciprocal balance between medial and lateral regions and their respective self- and environmental-related contents.

Philosophically, one may now raise the questions, from where do these intrinsic design features of the brain come, and how are they constructed? They may be the result of evolution, which would lead us back to the relationship between world and brain, the world–brain problem as stated above. The reciprocal nature of the balance may also be genetically predisposed and thus be part of the gene–brain problem. We need to understand the nature and origin of the brain's intrinsic design features in order to understand the various features of the mind, such as the reciprocal balance between internal (self and bodily) and external (environmental) mental contents. Accordingly, rather than questioning the nature of mind and how it is related to the brain, the philosopher may want to discuss the nature of the brain itself and its intrinsic design features. Viewed in an even larger picture, this perspective makes necessary the development of a philosophy of the brain (see Northoff, 2004) that may ultimately replace the hitherto dominating philosophy of mind—"minding the brain" (see Northoff, 2014d) rather than "minding the mind," one might say.

The Relational Self

I've demonstrated that depression can tell us much about the brain and how it is related to the mind and the mind–brain problem. One main component or feature of the mind is the self. The self may be conceived as a paradigmatic instance of the mind. To solve the problem of self will thus provide an answer to the mind–brain problem. For that reason I first conceptualize the self and later revisit the mind–brain problem.

What can depression teach us about the concept of self? As we've seen, depression can be broadly characterized by an increased self-focus accompanied by a decreased envi-

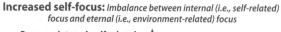

Increased self-focus: *Imbalance between internal (i.e., self-related) focus and eternal (i.e., environment-related) focus*

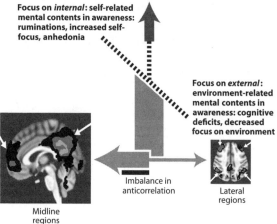

Focus on *internal*: **self-related mental contents in awareness: ruminations, increased self-focus, anhedonia**

Focus on *external*: **environment-related mental contents in awareness: cognitive deficits, decreased focus on environment**

Imbalance in anticorrelation

Lateral regions

Midline regions

Figure 4.1b ——————————————————

ronment focus. Patients experience an abnormally strong self-focus, often accompanied by rumination, and simultaneously feel disconnected from the environment. Both increased self-focus and decreased environment focus seem to be coupled and linked to each other in a negative, reciprocal way: If the one increases, the other decreases, and vice versa.

What does this reciprocal dependence between self-focus and environment focus tell us about the concept of self? Even the subject of experience, the self, cannot be considered independent and isolated from its environment. Instead of being detached from the environment, the self seems to be deeply embedded in it.

Based on these observations, one may want to characterize the self by its embeddedness in the environment, referred to as the embedded self. The concept of embeddedness describes the integration and linkage of the self to its respective context, the environment. Is this integration a necessary and thus intrinsic feature of the self as subject of experience? We currently do not know.

If it is the case, the self as subject of experience would be defined by its relation to the environment. This relation of the self to the environment seems to decrease, if not disappear altogether, in depression. These patients feel detached and disconnected from their environment, including from their partner, children, work, and social contacts. They feel that they can no longer relate to and connect with others; their focus shifts from the environment to themselves. We could say that the self of patients with depression suffers from *decreased embeddedness*: The self is isolated and detached from the environment.

Conceptually, this formulation implies that the concept of self must be defined as embedded in the environment. However, the exact characterization of the relational self remains unclear at this point. What constitutes and makes possible the relationship between self and environment, and thus the self as subject of experience? This question needs to be further investigated both empirically and conceptually in the future.

Mind–Brain Problem versus World–Brain Problem

What do the relational nature of self and its abnormal manifestation in depression tell us about the brain and its relationship to what philosophers call *mind*? As described previously, depression can be characterized as an imbalance in resting-state activity levels between midline and lateral cortical regions. We could now hypothesize that the medial–lateral resting-state imbalance is related to the imbalance between self-focus and environment focus in daily experience. However, more findings are necessary to support the assumption that the neuronal resting-state balance corresponds to the phenomenal balance between self and environment in lived experience. In short, we need to investigate the relationship between neuronal and phenomenal balances.

On the whole, depression can be characterized by imbalance between self and environment in experience, a phenomenal imbalance. This perspective suggests that the concept of self cannot be considered in an isolated way: It must be considered in relation to the environment; it is embedded and relational, as noted previously. At the same time, depression shows a neuronal imbalance in the resting-state activity between midline and lateral regions. Is the balance of the resting state between midline and lateral regions central for the embedded and relational self, the subject of experience?

If this is the case, the imbalance of the resting state between midline and lateral regions should be accompanied by changes in the self and its relation to the environment. As we saw described in the sections on increased-self focus and the decreased environment focus, this is indeed the case in depression. Most importantly, this imbalance tells us that the intrinsic activity of the brain must contain some information about its own relationship to the environment.

This brain's intrinsic activity and its information about

the self and its relationship to the environment have major implications for both empirical and conceptual considerations. Empirically, we would need to investigate how the brain's intrinsic activity couples with, and links itself to, the environment independent of, and prior to, the recruitment of specific functions (e.g., sensorimotor, cognitive). These functions all presuppose some kind of subject—the subject who experiences the respective functions. Therefore, the linkage of the brain's intrinsic activity to the environment must occur prior to, and independent of, these functions in order to make possible the constitution of a subject of experience as embedded and relational.

This conceptualization also has an important implication for how we should characterize the intrinsic activity of the brain. This intrinsic activity may no longer be considered as purely intrinsic, as opposed to the extrinsic environment. Instead, the seemingly intrinsic activity may be characterized by information integrated from the apparently extrinsic environment. In other words, the boundary between intrinsic and extrinsic becomes rather blurry and thus empirically implausible. The brain's resting-state activity is neither purely intrinsic and therefore inside the brain, nor is it purely extrinsic and thus outside the brain within the environment. Instead, the resting-state activity of the brain is both intrinsic and extrinsic at the same time, thereby making possible the continuous spatial–temporal flow within the triangular (i.e., relational) interconnections between brain, body, and environment. The resting-state activity can therefore be characterized as *relational*.

The resting state of the brain seems to be in charge of continuously constructing the relationship between brain, body, and environment. Abnormalities in the resting state lead to abnormalities in the relation between brain, body, and environment. There may be imbalance leading to increased self-focus and decreased environment focus, as in depression. And there may be a signification reduction in the resting-state activity that characterizes the vegetative state due to lack of energy. In that case the relation between brain, body, and environment can no longer be properly constructed, leading to the loss of consciousness.

What does the triangular relationship between self, body, and environment tell us about consciousness? It tells us that consciousness itself is based on the brain's resting-state activity and its continuous construction of the relation between brain, body, and environment. Put more simply, consciousness itself is relational, very much like the resting-state activity of the brain is relational. I postulated the same in the case of the self as relational. One may consequently say that mental features such as consciousness and sense of self are dependent upon the relation between brain, body, and environment, or more generally, the world–brain relation. If so, the mind–brain problem, as philosophers call it, may need to be reformulated as the world–brain problem: The question of the nature and origin of mental features can no longer be addressed by assuming some kind of mind and its relationship to the brain, but rather by conceiving the brain's relationship to the world—the world–brain relation, and more specifically, how the world is related to the resting-state activity of the brain. The problem of consciousness is consequently not one about the more general and basic problem of the mind–brain relationship but rather about the relationship between world and brain: the *world–brain problem*, as I call it. The world–brain problem raises the question about the shared features between world and brain and how they predispose the brain's resting-state activity to continuously construct relational interconnections to body and world. I postulate that investigating this question will shed a novel light on mental features such as sense of self and consciousness, which then can be traced to different yet unknown forms of the world–brain relationship.

Chapter 5

FEELING THE WORLD

───────── **PREVIEW** ─────────

*How can we experience
the world–brain relationship?*

───────────────────────────

In the last chapter I suggested that the mind–brain problem needs to be reformulated as a world–brain problem. The brain is closely linked to, and integrated within, the world and its various events, creating this world–brain relation. Most importantly, this world–brain relation is central for transforming the merely neuronal states of the brain into mental states such as sense of self and consciousness. In philosophical terms, this implies that we no longer need to assume a mind and question its relationship to the brain: The mind–brain problem becomes obsolete, as noted. Instead, we need to investigate the brain's relationship to the world, the world–brain relation (i.e., world-brain problem). How though can we provide further evidence for such a world–brain relation? Do we experience the relationship of the brain to the world in our consciousness? This is the moment where emotional feelings enter: the main topic in this chapter.

Emotional Feelings as Links to the World

Recall Judy, who became so depressed following a much-desired job promotion. She experienced extremely negative emotions, which led her into deep depression. Even worse, there was some point at which she experienced no emotional feelings at all. She perceived things around her, was aware of others and their smiles and passing comments, but she could no longer feel anything—neither happiness nor sadness. As she later recalled, this was the worst state she had ever experienced: feeling nothing, no emotion. At this point of feeling nothing whatsoever, she experienced herself to be completely disconnected and detached from others and the world in general. In short: no emotional feelings, no connection to the world.

Do emotional feelings signify our linkage to the world? Do we feel the brain's integration within the world, the world–brain relation, when we experience emotional feelings? First we need to consider what *emotions*, in general, and *emotional feelings*, in particular, are. There has been a long debate about emotions in philosophy, which recently has been complemented by intense research into the neural correlates of emotions. For instance, the neural activity in various subcortical regions of the brain (e.g., the amygdala) has been associated with specifically negative emotions such as sadness—and that very same region has also been observed to be hyperactive in depression. Positive emotions such as happiness have been linked to other subcortical regions (e.g., the striatum) that are closely linked to reward.

What are emotional feelings? The term *emotional feelings* refers to the subjective experience of emotions. You *perceive* happiness or sadness; these are emotions. But you also *feel* happy or sad; the feeling is your subjective experience of the emotion. We recall that consciousness is determined by the "what it is like" quality—the subjective experience of a particular event or content. Emotional feelings are the subjective experience, the conscious awareness of an emotion. You feel happy; you feel sad; you feel gloomy. It is this feeling that you experience; it is the subjective component in emotional feeling. Those subjective components of emotions and how they signify our relationship to the world, the world–brain relation, rather than their objective components, the bare emotions, are the focus in this chapter.

How can *emotional feelings* be distinguished from mere *emotions*? As in the case of self and consciousness, it is always useful to return to the history of philosophy to help us understand where our current definitions come from and why *emotional feelings* are defined in this way rather than in some other way. Once again, we turn to René Descartes.

Descartes considered emotions to be a subclass of perceptions that may have their origin in either the body or the soul. Although he associated emotions with the movements of the life spirit, he saw this linkage as contingent, such that emotions could be considered as mental rather than as purely physical. However, he recognized that emotions remain impossible without the body; the soul cannot freely determine its emotions. Another hallmark of emotions that Descartes noted is that they are accessible only subjectively, in our first-person perspectives and in our mental states, and therefore cannot be observed from the outside by others in a third-person perspective. Descartes's association of emotions with both body and soul remains a problem today, as the problem of classifying emotions in a new context of hybrid conceptualization continues.

There has been much discussion about the relationship between emotions and emotional feelings in the contemporary philosophy of emotions (e.g., see De Sousa, 2007). Some authors (e.g., James, 1890; see Schachter & Singer, 1962, for details) argue that emotions are simply a class of feelings that must be distinguished from mere sensation and proprioception—one's own, individual perception—by their experience. Emotional feelings are then at the very core of emotions, with emotions depending on emotional feelings in what is often called the "feeling theories" of emotions.

Emotions can also be defined by their objects, rather than by the feelings of the emotions. For instance, if I am afraid of a dog, which gives me anxiety, the dog is the object of my emotion in that particular circumstance. It does not matter whether the object is real or virtual as long as it is associated with specific emotions. In this sense, emotions are defined by the objects that elicit them.

Yet another way to define emotions is in terms of evaluation or appraisal. The object of an emotion is not, by itself, intrinsically emotional; we experience a certain emotion in response to the object by the way we appraise it. For instance, the dog is appraised as fearsome, but it is *my belief* about the dog, rather than the dog itself, that underlies and triggers my emotion of anxiety. Such focus on appraisal led to the development of cognitive or appraisal theories of emotions.

There has been plenty of discussion in philosophy, psychology, and neuroscience about what exactly emotions and emotional feelings are, with the different theories oscillating between brain-, body-, environment-, or mind-based accounts.

Several questions arise. Do emotional feelings result

from our brain's neural processes, the perception of the body's interoceptive stimuli, or from the exteroceptive stimuli from the environment? In short, are emotional feelings neurally, bodily, or environmentally based? We need to investigate these questions in order to understand what emotional feelings are and how they are related to the world–brain problem. If, for instance, emotional feelings are merely neural and "reside" solely within the brain itself, they would not show any connection to the world. In that case emotional feelings will not tell us anything about the world–brain relation. If, in contrast, they are environmental and span across and link brain, body, and environment, then emotional feelings may provide experiential access to the world and may then be assumed to signify our relationship to the world: the world–brain relation.

"Having an Emotion" versus "Feeling an Emotion"

The creator of the theory of evolution, naturalist Charles Darwin (1809–1882), believed that motor behaviors such as facial expressions and posture convey an organism's response to events and to objects in the environment. Our gestures and postures convey our emotions. Watch an Italian person talking, for instance; intense gesturing with rapid hand movements convey the strong emotions felt by that person. (Of course, culture and the respective environmental context dictate whether effusive gesturing is a good or bad way to be.) This is very much in line with the observation that emotion-specific motor behavior is accompanied by subjective experience—that is, emotional feeling—of the respective emotion. For instance, if a person inhibits or suppresses the gestures (the motor behavior), he or she would also supress the associated emotional feeling. Consider the case of mania, the opposite extreme of depression. While suffering from depression, people barely move and ultimately do not feel anything anymore; in contrast, manic patients, who are extremely happy, pace around the room at high speed. Their extreme and abnormal feeling of happiness finds its outlet in their motor behavior, the abnormally fast pacing and walking.

These observations indicate that sensorimotor function seems to be involved in constituting and expressing emotional feelings and emotions. Due to our sensory and motor functions and their respective neural correlates, we may feel something, whereas in the absence of motor behavior, we may no longer feel anything—as in depression, exemplified by Judy, who no longer experienced any feelings. Our feelings, therefore, seem to be closely linked to the body and its sensorimotor functions. More technically put, *emotional feelings are apparently embodied.*

How can emotional feelings be embodied and be linked to the body's sensory and motor functions? William James, the famous psychologist, partnered with a colleague, Carl Lange, and developed the famous James–Lange theory of emotional feelings. This theory defined feelings as perceptions of physiological changes in the body, thus basing them on sensorimotor and vegetative functions. When we perceive the physiological changes in our bodies, such as changes in heart rate, we develop emotional feelings—for instance, anxiety when the heart rate accelerates. In the context of this theory, depression would be seen as an abnormal perception of the body—which indeed is the case. Patients with depression, like Judy, often develop strong somatic symptoms, perceiving their bodies and the associated physiological changes in an abnormal way that leads them subjectively to feel pain or anxiety, even if the heart rate remains objectively normal.

The James–Lange theory was originally a psychological theory, with the aim to explain how the perception of one's own bodily signals translates into emotional feelings. Modern versions of this theory resurface in current neuroscientific models of emotion as, for instance, in Damasio's (1999, 2010) theory. Damasio considers emotion and feeling to be in close relation to the perception of bodily changes. Physiological bodily changes such as fluctuations in heart rate are reported to be registered in specific brain regions in the deeper parts of the subcortex, the *first-order neural structures*. These include the brainstem and midbrain regions (e.g., periaqueductal gray, tectum), and the amygdala, which are all involved in processing the inputs the body sends to the brain. These regions account for the induction of emotions, which, according to Damasio, remain unconscious, so that one may speak of "having an emotion" at this level.

Importantly, merely "having an emotion" does not include any emotional feelings—that is, the subjective experience of the emotions. For that subjective experience to occur, the neural activity in the subcortical regions, the first-order neural structures, needs to be incorporated and reprocessed by other brain regions, the second-order neural structures. These regions include the cingulate gyrus, thalamic nuclei, the somatosensory cortex, and the superior colliculi. The reprocessing of the emotion in these regions assigns the "feeling of an emotion" (Damasio, 1999). These second-order neural structures allow us to perceive what has been registered about the physiological somatic changes taking place in first-order neural structures. It is this perception that induces emotional feelings, which Damasio calls "feeling an emotion."

Taken together, Damasio assumes a two-stage process. There is first the generation of an emotion, the "having an emotion" by first-order neural structures, when processing the body's input in the brain. That input remains completely unconscious and is therefore not associated with an emotional feeling. In order for consciousness and thus a feeling to be assigned to the primarily unconscious emotion, the initial neural activity needs to be reprocessed in other regions. The emotion is then linked to consciousness and thus to a feeling, the emotional feeling.

To "Have an Emotion" Is to "Feel an Emotion and the World"

Neuroscientist Jaak Panksepp does not assume a two-stage process (Panksepp, 1998a, 1998b, 2007a, 2007b, 2011a, 2011b). He assumes that the neural activity in the first-order structures is already, by itself, associated with emotional feelings. As soon as these regions become active by, for instance, processing the sensory input from the body and the motor output to the body, emotional feelings are generated. Subcortical regions such as the periaqueductal gray are central here. They process the linkage between sensory input from body and environment and at the same time link it to motor functions. Emotional feelings are assumed to result from such linkage between bodily and environmental sensory input to the body's motor functions.

Importantly, unlike in Damasio's theory, there is no two-stage distinction between unconscious emotions—between "having an emotion" and the conscious experience of "feeling of an emotion." "No such distinction exists in the brain," Panksepp (1998a) would most likely say, then continue with: "Any neural activity in the brain and its processing of sensory inputs from both world and body is always already associated with a feeling."

Why is the difference between Damasio's and Panksepp's view of emotional feeling important in our context? Damasio associates emotional feelings with the reprocessing or second-order processing of the bodily input. In that case emotional feelings are not directly connected to body (and environment) but at best indirectly. For Panksepp, any input from body and world into the brain directly leads to emotional feelings. Any changes in body and environment induce neural activity changes in primarily subcortical regions that are related to emotional feelings.

Hence, metaphorically put, Panksepp would say that we feel the brain's relation to body and world. Emotional feelings are the manifestation of the world–brain relation in our consciousness. Damasio, in contrast, would say that the world–brain relation is processed but not directly felt as such. Any emotional feeling does not signify the world–brain relation itself, but rather additional elaboration within the brain and its second-order neural structures.

Who is right: Damasio or Panksepp? If Panksepp is right, emotional feelings signify the world–brain relation such that we continuously experience the world and its relationship to our brain in our emotional feelings. Emotional feelings would then be existential, as they signify our existence within the world, our "*Dasein*" as the German philosopher Martin Heidegger said at the beginning of the 20th century. If, in contrast, Damasio is right, emotional feelings signify the brain itself—what it does and what it adds to the mere emotions—more or less independent of its relationship to the world. In that case emotional feelings do not tell us a tale about the world–brain relation but only about the brain itself.

Are Emotional Feelings the Inner Cognitive Elaboration of the Brain?

How can Damasio and Panksepp account for the distinct types of emotional feelings such as sadness, happiness, gloominess? The lack of specificity concerning distinct emotions has often been criticized in theories such as the James–Lange theory. Autonomic, or involuntary, bodily changes like arousal are rather unspecific reactions that do not allow distinguishing between discrete emotions. How can one and the same input from the body, such as the heart rate, lead to emotions so different as anxiety and happiness?

This criticism has been furnished by the Schachter & Singer (1962) experiments. These researchers stimulated the subjects' autonomic nervous systems by administering drugs such as epinephrine (i.e., adrenaline). They then placed the subjects in different rooms: In one room, a happy actor was present, whereas in the other room was an angry actor. How did the subjects experience their drug-induced increase in arousal in these different rooms? Interestingly, their emotional feeling strongly depended on the presence of the respective actor. The same increased arousal was associated with an emotional feeling of anger in the angry actor's room, whereas in the presence of the happy actor, subjects experienced happiness. Hence, the increased arousal itself was not associated with a specific emotional feeling but rather depended upon the context.

This experiment shed some doubt on the James–Lange theory and its claim that emotional feelings can be traced back to the perception of the sensory input from the body. Where, though, do emotional feelings come from? There must be an additional function beyond the merely sensory function that allows the generating of emotional feelings. What are these additional functions? Many authors assume them to be cognitive functions, which leads us now to the cognitive theories of emotional feelings.

Feeling and Cognition

Cognitive approaches associate emotional feelings with abstract cognitive functions (e.g., linguistic function or working memory) rather than sensorimotor (and vegetative) functions as related to the body. For example, Rolls and colleagues (Rolls, 2000; Rolls, Tovee, & Panzeri, 1999) assume that higher-order linguistic thought processing is essential for the occurrence of consciousness and consequently for the emergence of emotional feelings. LeDoux (2003) considers working memory to be crucial for consciousness. Both Rolls and LeDoux argue that primarily the brain constructs an emotion, which is then taken up by cognitive functions. The cognitive functions further elaborate the objective emotions in such way that they are associated with a subjective feeling, the emotional feeling. As in Damasio's theory, Rolls and LeDoux both assume a two-stage process with a distinction between emotion and emotional feeling, the latter building upon the former. The only difference among these three researchers is that Rolls and LeDoux associate the second process, the generation of emotional feelings, with cognitive functions, whereas Damasio assumes more of an intermediate process (between sensory and cognitive functions).

What does a cognitive approach to emotional feelings look like? There is neural activity related to the emotion itself, independent of and prior to any feeling, like neural processing of disgusting scenes in various regions of the brain, including subcortical areas like the amygdala. No feeling will arise yet at this early and most basic stage. The same processing is then also extended to cortical regions such as the prefrontal and parietal cortices that associate the mere subcortical emotion processing of the disgusting pictures with various cognitive functions such as working memory and attention. Associating the hitherto subcortically unconscious emotional stimulus processing with these cognitive functions lifts the former into consciousness: One now experiences or feels disgust. Hence emotional feeling (as distinguished from mere emotional processing) is closely linked to cognitive functions (LeDoux, 2003). Though these approaches differ in various aspects, they all account for emotional feeling by higher-order processing and the related cognitive functions.

How can the cognitive functions account for different emotional feelings? The cognitive approach assumes that cognitive functions evaluate and appraise the contents in different ways. We may appraise or evaluate an emotion as happy or sad depending on the context (as shown in the Schachter and Singer experiment). Hence it is the appraisal or evaluation that allows us to distinguish different kinds of emotions. Philosophers such as Scherer and Solomon therefore speak of what they call the "appraisal theory of emotions" (see Northoff, 2012, for an extensive discussion). The different kinds of emotional feelings reflect our appraisal processes and their associated cognitive functions.

How does the appraisal theory of emotions fit with the world–brain relation? Appraisal reflects the higher-order cognitive functions of the brain and its inner elaboration rather than the brain's relation to the world. Emotional feeling, in the appraisal theory, signifies what philosophers have described as the mind, which is currently referred to as cognition and cognitive function. The appraisal theory of emotion in philosophy and its cognitive variants in neuroscience can thus be considered to continue and extend the Cartesian philosophical tradition into the 21st century. What Descartes characterized as dualism between mind and brain resurfaces in our times as the dualism between "feeling an emotion" and "having an emotion," which empirically is related to the difference between cognitive and sensory functions.

Like the mind in Descartes's philosophy, the brain is here associated with cognitive functions that operate independently of the brain's relation to the world. All that the world–brain relation can provide is mere sensory input, which is, at best, important for emotion but not for emotional feeling. For emotional feeling to occur, however, requires the cognitive functions and their elaborations within the brain itself. Emotional feelings are here detached from the world and exclusively associated with the inner elaboration of the brain's cognitive functions.

Does such a cognitive model of emotional feelings reflect our experience? Recall Judy: She was depressed and felt sadness. She was not able to experience any joy or happiness in the world at all; not only was she sad and gloomy, but in her eyes so was the whole world. Her sadness was not limited to herself; its ubiquitousness is what made her depression so painful. It is this inclusion of the whole world that makes the depression ultimately existential and often drives these patients into suicidal thoughts, if not into suicide itself.

Emotional feelings cannot be detached and dissociated from the world. They are not located in the cognitive elaborations of our brain. They signify the world–brain relation, and, more specifically, our (or our self's) relation to other persons (and their selves). How can we account for the fact that emotional feelings are relational, signifying the world–brain relation? Let's consider a particular region in the brain, the insula, which has been closely associated with emotional feeling, to explore this question.

The Role of the Insula and the Experience of Feelings

Brain, body, or environment—where do emotional feelings reside? We have the choice between the body and its interoceptive stimuli, the brain and its cognitive functions, and exteroceptive stimuli from the environment. Besides her abnormally negative emotional feelings, Judy also complained about abnormal bodily sensations, chest pain, stomach pressure, and tightness when breathing. But no physical problems could be found in her heart, lungs, and stomach. The psychiatrist finally traced these bodily, or somatic, symptoms back to the depression, which can cause these kinds of symptoms. How closely are emotional feelings related to the body and its somatic functions? In this section we will see that they are very closely related indeed.

Traditionally, as we have seen above, emotional feelings

were characterized by sensorimotor functions and, as such, were seen as closely related to one's perception of one's body, presupposing what is called interoceptive awareness. This means that interoceptive stimuli stemming from one's own body, rather than exteroceptive stimuli from the environment, may be central in mediating emotional feelings. Neuroscientific investigations of emotional feelings have focused on the neuronal processing of interoceptive stimuli in the body and our awareness of them.

Imaging studies using fMRI investigated neural activity during interoceptive stimuli processing, such as changes in blood pressure or heart rate (Medford & Critchley, 2010; Wiebking et al., 2014). These studies observed neural activity changes in the right insula, the anterior cingulate cortex extending from supragenual to dorsal regions (SACC–DACC), and the amygdala. This led to the assumption that the right insula and the SACC–DACC integrally represent autonomic and visceral responses that are transferred from the spinal cord through the midbrain, the hypothalamus, and the thalamic–cortical pathway to the right insular cortex.

Based on these results, the neuroscientist Bud Craig assumes the right insula to be crucially involved: It receives autonomic and visceral input from lower centers and reprocesses (or *re*represents) the interoceptive body state in an integrated way (Craig, 2002, 2003, 2004, 2009a, 2009b, 2010a, 2010b, 2010c, 2011). This process allows the insula to give rise to a "mental image of one's physical state." That, in turn, according to Craig, provides the basis for subjective awareness of emotional feeling and one's self as "material me."

If these regions mediate interoceptive processing of the

body, the question of their role in emotional feeling arises. Critchley and colleagues (Critchley, Wiens, Rotshtein, Ohman, & Dolan, 2004) asked subjects to evaluate whether their heartbeat, as interoceptive input, was synchronous or asynchronous when compared to a tone, an exteroceptive input. Subjects had to direct their attention to either their own heart or the tone when asked to count the number of heartbeats or tones presented. This methodology allowed the researchers to directly compare interoceptive- and exteroceptive-directed attention (i.e., internally or externally directed attention) (Critchley et al., 2004).

What did Critchley and colleagues observe in the insula during intero- and exteroceptive attention? Interoceptive attention to one's own heartbeat increased activity in the right insula (as well as the SACC–DACC and the DMPFC), whereas exteroceptive attention to the tone suppressed activity in the very same region. This finding indicates that the insula seems to distinguish between internally and externally guided attention, with the former increasing its activity and the latter decreasing it. Most interestingly, activity especially in the right insula during heartbeat detection also correlated with emotional feelings of anxiety: the more activity in the insula, the better the heartbeat detection and the lower the degree of anxiety. If, in contrast, heartbeat detection was poor, activity in the insula was low, which in turn led to increased emotional feelings of anxiety.

This experimental research can be further supported by observations of patients with depression. Patients like Judy perform extremely poorly in detecting their own heartbeats. They subjectively experience their own heartbeat as racing much faster than it objectively measures. As we observed

(Wiebking et al., 2010), this abnormal heartbeat detection is related to decreased activity in the insula and to the abnormal emotional feelings such as anxiety in these patients.

What is the relevance of this research for us? The insula seems to be central in mediating the balance between intero- and exteroceptive inputs from body and environment and how we pay attention to them. This function puts the insula and its neural activity right at the interface between body and environment in the neural processing of the brain. One cannot say that the insula and its neural activity are detached from the body and the environment and their respective inputs. Instead, the insula seems to mediate their balance in our attention and ultimately in our experience. Most importantly, the modulation of the balance between body and environment is closely associated with emotional feelings such as the feeling of anxiety. This association suggests that emotional feelings signify the balance or relation between body and environment. For this reason emotional feelings must be conceived as truly relational in a rather literal sense. How can we further support such a claim on the basis of the brain? That is the purpose of the subsequent sections.

Balance Between Body and Environment

Are emotional feelings intero- or exteroceptive? Are they related to the body or the environment? The results from the research seem to suggest that emotional feelings are closely related to interoceptive awareness and thus to the body, rather than to either environment or cognition. We have to be careful, though. Neither the applied tasks probing emotional feelings and interoceptive awareness nor the regions themselves can be characterized by interoceptive processing alone. Let's start with the tasks and then shed some light on the connectivity patterns among the regions.

None of the tasks or paradigms employed in the cited research investigated interoceptive stimuli in isolation from exteroceptive stimuli, but rather in relation to them. Critchley and colleagues (2004), for instance, investigated heartbeat perception in relation to auditory tones as exteroceptive stimuli, whereas others directly compared both conditions with each other. Neural activity changes assumed to be specific for interoceptive awareness thus reflect a relation or dynamic balance between intero- and exteroceptive processing rather than isolated interoceptive stimulus processing (more or less) independent of exteroceptive stimulus processing.

The assumption of such intero–exteroceptive balance is also supported by the connectivity pattern of the respective regions. The insula receives considerable input and connections from the deeper subcortical regions that process the interoceptive input from the rest of the body. In addition to such input, the insula also receives direct input from the five sensory regions (auditory, visual, gustatory, sensorimotor, and olfactory) that process input from the environment. If so, neural activity in the insula reflects an intero–exteroceptive balance rather than stimuli from the body alone.

There are other ways to support the assumption of intero–exteroceptive balance, rather than interoceptive stimuli determining neural activity in the insula. Patients with somatoform disorder (in which patients experience physical, i.e., somatic, symptoms that cannot be traced to any underlying medical condition) or depression often show strong somatic symptoms with the subjective perception of pain, pounding heartbeat, and so on, despite the lack of any objective abnormalities. This was the case with Judy, our depressed patient from Chapter 4, who also showed strong somatic symptoms with chest pain, stomach pressure, and constricted breathing. How do these symptoms arise? We investigated both groups of patients, those with somatoform disorder and those with clinical depression, using fMRI during the heartbeat detection task to find out (de Greck et al., 2012; Wiebking et al., 2010).

Although we expected to see abnormally increased insula activity during the interoceptive task of heartbeat detection, it turned out to be normal and did not differ from healthy subjects. However, the insula and auditory cortical activity, which we expected to be normal during the auditory tone detection, was significantly decreased. The patients seemed unable to properly process stimuli from the environment during this task. This discovery shifts the postulated intero–exteroceptive balance toward its interoceptive pole, with the (relatively stronger) interoceptive input dominating the contents in awareness. The intero–exteroceptive imbalance on the neural level subsequently leads to an imbalance between bodily and environmental contents in awareness: One's own body becomes the predominating content in awareness at the expense of environmental contents—which is exactly what both somatoform and depressed patients report.

Aha! Now matters become somewhat clearer. Patients with depression feel detached and isolated from the world, just as Judy reported feeling disconnected from her relatives and all others. The invisible bond to the world that we continuously experience is disrupted in depression. Patients with depression have no motivation at all to interact with that very same world and withdraw socially, turning inward, as manifested in the increased self-focus.

These findings shed light on that disconnection from the world. For some yet unknown reason, the exteroceptive stimuli from the environment are no longer properly processed and do not induce much activity change in the brain. The intero–exterocpetive balance consequently shifts toward the interoceptive/internal activity changes at the expense of the exteroceptive processing. The resulting emotional feelings no longer signify the world–brain relation but only, in broad terms, the brain–self relationship, as it is manifested in the increased self-focus.

Emotional Feelings Are Relational

What do the intero–exteroceptive balance on the neural level and the balance between bodily and environmental contents on the level of awareness entail for emotional feelings? Do emotional feelings reside in the brain, the body, or the environment? The empirical data suggest that none of the three holds. Emotional feelings are neither in the body nor can they be reduced to perception of the body (i.e., interoceptive awareness) as mediated by neural activity in the brain.

As we have seen, neural activity in the insula and the associated regions during both interoceptive awareness and the experience of emotional feelings is characterized by an intero–exteroceptive balance rather than by isolated interoceptive processing. What is processed in the insula is not the body alone but its relation to the environment. In fact, we are not aware of the body, distinct and independent from the environment. Instead, we are aware of our bodies, including our heartbeats, relative to what happens in the environment in the same way we are aware of the environment relative to what happens in our bodies. We experience our bodies in relation to our respective environmental contexts; this relationship is individual and makes it possible to experience that body as "my" body (rather than somebody else's body).

Usually our awareness of both body and environment are in synchrony, showing balance with each other in our awareness. If, for example, my awareness of my body increases, the environmental contents around me recede into the background. The same happens the other way around as well: If the environmental contents—for example, the exteroceptive input—predominate in my awareness, the concurrent awareness of my body's total interoceptive input into the insula and related regions decreases. This is the "normal" shifting of the intero–exteroceptive, or body–environment, balance we experience daily in our awareness.

What do these findings imply for emotional feelings? That they are the result of the intero–exteroceptive balance. They are truly relational rather than just intero- or exteroceptive. Patients with somatoform or depressive disorders become anxious when feeling their own hearts pounding and stuttering, even though, objectively, their hearts work perfectly fine. Emotional feelings can be characterized neither as the domain of the body nor of the environment. Instead, they are about balance: the relation between intero- and exteroceptive input and the following relation between bodily and environmental contents. Nor are feelings merely in the brain, as Damasio and the proponents of cognitive theories assume. Emotional feelings are not merely the products of inner neurocognitive elabora-

tions of the brain. Instead they reflect the balance and continuous adjustment between the brain's neural activity (as
in the insula) in relation to body and environment. In short,
emotional feelings can be located neither in the brain nor in
body and environment.

Neuroscientists and philosophers alike seem to
approach emotional feelings incorrectly with discrete categories: as brain, body, *or* environment; as neurocognitive
or intero- *or* exteroceptive. Instead of segregating these
domains, we may need to conceive of their *inter*relationship, their balance, which may allow us to pinpoint the
origin of emotional feelings. Emotional feelings reflect a
balance between brain, bodily, and environmental input.
And it is the brain that makes possible and constructs this
balance. Emotional feelings are our experience of this balance, which I describe as a *world–brain relation*. Taken
in this sense, emotional feelings are not only of interest to
psychologists and neuroscientists but also to philosophers.
They provide us with access to the world itself as it is
related to us and our brains. Although they did not yet recognize the importance of the brain and world–brain relation, existentialist philosophers such as Martin Heidegger
(1927/2010) and Matthew Ratcliffe (2008) pointed out that
emotional feelings are a key to the world. That is the topic
in the following section.

Existential Feelings and the World

Searching for the different kinds of balances, like the one
between intero- and exteroceptive stimuli in the neural processing of the brain—this is the lesson that the neurophilosophy of emotional feelings can teach the neuroscientist.

Look for conceptualizations and models that do not fall prey to the alternative between body and environment—this is the lesson the philosopher can learn from the neurophilosophy of emotional feeling.

Existentialist philosophers such as the famous German philosopher Martin Heidegger (1889–1976) and present-day British philosopher Matthew Ratcliffe (2008) sketch a view of emotional feelings that is compatible with the neurophilosophical insights. (Contemporary novelists such as Siri Hustvedt also have a deep sense of the existential character of our emotional feelings as signifying the world around us rather than just some inner musings of a mind or merely the inner cognitive elaborations of a brain.) These philosophers claim that emotional feelings are *existential* in that they always occur against the backdrop of the world, the being-in-the-world or "*Dasein*," as Heidegger says. Emotional feelings are, as they would probably say, the way of "finding ourselves in the world" or "subjective engagements within the world." For instance, different existential feelings (e.g., separation, belonging, power, control, anxiety) characterize different relations to the world. If so, the body itself may be considered as the only medium through which feelings can be constituted. Feelings are the relation between the person/body and environment rather than some perception of either bodily or environmental changes; in other terms, feelings represent the relation between the person and the world, a relationship experienced in terms of emotional feelings.

Why and how do we experience emotional feelings in such a relational and existential way? Neurophilosophers may want to argue that that is simply the way the brain is designed: It does not allow us to process interoceptive stimuli from the body alone, independent of the exteroceptive

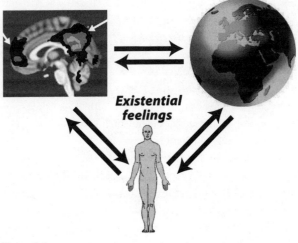

Existential feelings

Figure 5.1 _____

stimuli from the environment. And vice versa: Our brains
can't process stimuli from the environment without the
interoceptive stimuli from our bodies. All the brain can do is
process the balance between both, the intero–exteroceptive
balance, which in our awareness is manifested as the balance between body and environment.

This line of thinking brings us to an interesting thought
experiment for the philosopher. What would it mean for
emotional feelings if the brain were designed in a different
way, namely, by the isolated and independent processing of
both intero- and exteroceptive stimuli? Would we still have
emotional feelings? This is for the philosophers to decide—
but I warn them, they may remain unable to decide this
issue on the basis of their very own brains, which also bear
the above-mentioned design. Of course, it isn't really rele-

vant for us whether philosophers can decide this issue or not. All we need to know is how the brain processes intero- and exteroceptive stimuli and generates emotional feelings. If we know that, we can get a grip on our own emotional feelings and better help those patients suffering from soma- toform and depressive disorders who are haunted by abnor- mal emotional feelings.

The existentialist philosophers got it right: Emotional feelings signify our relation to the world and, put into more dramatic terms, our existence as such. That is why an alter- ation of emotional feelings, as occurs in depression, is so painful and changes the whole existence of patients like Judy. The existentialist philosophers set emotional feel- ings into the context of the world. However, they left unad- dressed why and how emotional feelings are intrinsically linked to the world. This is the moment where the brain and its relation to the world, the world–brain relation, reenters our purview. As shown in preceding material, it is the brain and, more specifically, certain regions within it such as the insula, that establish a direct relation between the neural stimuli within the brain itself, the bodily or interoceptive stimuli, and the environmental or exteroceptive stimuli. The findings further show that the construction of this threefold interrelation between brain, body, and environ- ment is directly associated with emotional feelings. Emo- tional feelings are consequently relational.

In a nutshell, emotional feelings provide access to the world and our existence as part of that very same world. They signify the world–brain relation in our experience. Emotional feelings are our experiential placeholder for the world–brain relation, and, at the same time, they ground our existence. In short, emotional feelings are existential. That is why a deep and basic alteration of emotional feelings, as in depression, affects the person's experience of his or her very existence and relation to the world.

Person–Body Dialogue about Emotional Feelings

To close this chapter on the relationship between body and emotional feelings, here is an imagined dialogue between a person, who experiences emotional feelings, and a body, if it were able to speak by itself.

PERSON: I am a person. Who are you?

BODY: I am your body. I am surprised that you do not know me.

PERSON: No, I have never met you.

BODY: How is that possible? I am always with you, yet you do not notice me?

PERSON: How can I notice you? I am too busy experiencing and being aware of my feelings, my emotional feelings.

BODY: What do you mean by that?

PERSON: Of course you would ask this question. Only a body without any emotional feelings could ask this. You seem to be devoid of emotional feelings.

BODY: That does not answer my question!

PERSON: You would have to feel them, the emotional feelings, to know exactly what is meant by emotional feelings.

BODY: Excuse me. As much as I appreciate your subjective experience of emotional feelings, I do not need to experience or feel them in order to know what they are. That would mean that one would need to be, for instance, a table in order to understand what a table is. I am almost certain, though, that you understand what a table is without being a table yourself. Or does my visual perception deceive me at this point?

PERSON: Be assured, your perception is perfect, I am not a table. And despite that, I nevertheless know what a table is. You are right in that point, but your line of thinking here does not apply to emotional feelings.

BODY: Why not?

PERSON: Because they are emotional feelings which are subjective and not objective, like a table, for instance.

BODY: What the hell do you mean by *subjective*? That seems to me a rather elusive term for something you remain unable to determine by itself.

PERSON: What a friendly irony! That is exactly the point where you remain unable to follow me. *Subjective* means that something is experienced and accessed only by persons in general and, more detailed, by a specific person—as, for instance, by me. I am a person and I am a specific person—a particular, individual person.

BODY: That does not sound as complicated as you apparently would like to make it. OK, you characterize emotional feelings as subjective and attribute such subjectivity to persons in general and, moreover, to particular persons. What is so complicated about that?

PERSON: Even if you understand that point, you will not be able to understand what subjectivity and, hence, emotional feelings are about.

BODY: Why not?

PERSON: Because you are not a person in general, but a body. Nor are you individual.

BODY: What do you mean? I am not individual—meaning, I am not an individual body?

PERSON: Yes, exactly that. You are a mere physical object devoid of any individuality.

BODY: Now I am almost offended. You reserve for yourself this individuality.

PERSON: Yes, correct. That individuality is, for instance, manifested in the different emotional feelings like sadness, happiness, and joy I am able to feel, and the fact that my feelings differ from other persons' feelings.

BODY: But how are these emotional feelings, including their individual character, generated? Where do they come from?

PERSON: That must be the mind.

BODY: Do not tell me such a fairy tale! I am not a 5-year-old. There is no mind; there is nothing but the body. That is the fact of life and also of your existence as a person. You are body and your body harbors your brain, which may be central in generating your emotional feelings.

PERSON: OK, putting my assumption of a mind reluctantly aside for didactic purposes, I nevertheless want to raise the question of how the brain and the rest of the body are related to each other during emotional feelings.

BODY: Why do you ask that question?

PERSON: Because all my emotional feelings go along with changes in my body. When I am afraid, I sweat and my heart rate accelerates, but when I am happy and joyful, then neither am I sweaty, nor do I experience an increase in my heart rate. Hence, emotional feelings must be somehow related to the body.

BODY: Yes, of course, because I, as body, mediate everything. I am like a channel everyone has to walk through in order to get from the train station to the city center, so to speak.

PERSON: The body and its interoceptive stimuli are nothing but a channel to get from the brain, as the train station, to the environment, as the city center? No, that cannot be true. The bodily nature of my emotional feelings is so strong that I cannot imagine my body as being merely a relay station. My emotional feelings must have their origin in my body. My body harbors my emotional feelings. All there is to my emotional feelings is bodily.

BODY: Now I am puzzled—only slightly, of course. Just minutes ago you claimed that the person with a mind harbors your sacred emotional feelings. And now you suddenly switch to me as body.

PERSON: You are right and wrong. It is indeed you, the body, to which I am referring. But it is not that body to which you think I am referring; it is not the physical body I observe from the outside. Instead, it is from the *inside* of the body, as the person subjectively experiences his or her own body—this is what phenomenological philosophers describe as the "lived body."

BODY: So emotional feelings are nothing but the body-based signaling of a specific relationship between the brain and the rest of the body? There is no city center, only a train station and a tunnel? If there is no city center, though, the direction of the tunnel—where it leads to—remains open and unclear.

PERSON: What do you mean?

BODY: Your beloved emotional feelings must be directed *toward* something. In the same way a tunnel must lead to somewhere, your emotional feelings must refer to something outside themselves. Your emotional feelings have, for instance, a specific object: the dog that makes you anxious, the darkness in the tunnel that makes you

scared, the \$1 million you won and are happy about—
these are all objects, be they real and thus physical, or
purely mental, to which your emotional feelings refer.
How does this *intentionality*, as philosophers term it,
come about?

PERSON: Are you saying that what the city center is to the
tunnel, the environment and its different objects must be
to emotional feelings?

BODY: Exactly that.

PERSON: That analogy implies that we cannot determine
emotional feelings solely by the body while leaving the
environment aside, since that would mean neglecting the
city center and letting the tunnel end nowhere?

BODY: Yes. We need to understand how it is possible for the
body to serve as the tunnel leading from the train station, the brain, to the city center, the environment.

PERSON: And by taking the path in the tunnel from the train
station to the city center, we experience emotional feelings? I can certainly subscribe to that, given my claustro-
phobia in dark, narrow rooms!

Chapter 6

THE WORLD–BRAIN DISRUPTION IN SCHIZOPHRENIA

 PREVIEW

What happens if the world–brain relation is disrupted?

Contemporary philosophy is much concerned with the mind and how it relates to the brain, the mind–brain problem. Relying on evidence from neuroscience and psychiatry, I suggested in Chapter 4 that we need to replace the mind–brain problem/relation with what I describe as the *world–brain problem/relation* to encompass how the brain links to, and integrates within, the world (and thereby makes possible, i.e., predisposes mental features like consciousness). Further evidence for the world–brain relation was discussed in Chapter 5: We experience the brain's relation to the world in terms of our emotional feelings; we *feel* our relation to the world and how we, on the basis of the brain, are integrated and exist within that very same world. What happens if that very same world–brain relation is disrupted? This, as I suggest, is the case in another psychiatric disorder, schizophrenia, which can serve as paradigmatic example of world–brain disruption. As in preceding chapters, first I present a purely fictive though paradigmatic case history.

CASE EXAMPLE

Childhood and Personality

Since typical behavioral and personality features often precede the outbreak of schizophrenic symptoms, I first provide a description of Andrew prior to his illness.

Andrew is a 19-year-old college freshman. He is still in his first year of college, for which he moved from San Francisco to Boston. Being the middle child of a family with three kids, he, unlike his siblings, was always a loner. When his siblings were playing with kids in the neighborhood, he stayed away, preferring to play by himself. The more people around him, the more he withdrew, preferring to be socially isolated. He darkly remembers how one of his aunts once said that he reminded her of his uncle, whom family members only vaguely mentioned and who ended up in a psychiatric hospital somewhere.

As he grew up it became clear that Andrew, though rather withdrawn socially, was highly intelligent. He excelled especially in mathematics and physics, for which he developed a strong predilection. Usually he was the best at his school and won several competitions in his home state of California, as well as second prize in a nationwide competition for young mathematicians. The latter wasn't a happy memory for Andrew, though. The worst of it, he recalls, was not the competition, which, had he been calmer, he could have easily won. No, the worst for him was sitting with all the people in the airplane on the flight from San Francisco to Washington, DC. During the whole competition he was dreading the return flight and preoccupied with how to avoid people.

His extraordinary skills in mathematics and physics earned him an award and admission to Harvard University in Cambridge, Massachusetts, for which anybody else would have jumped to the ceiling. Andrew did not. In truth, he really didn't care much. Instead, he was preoccupied with details: how he would get there, yet another terrible and overloaded flight where he had to be in close contact with others; how to deal with all the students and the dormitory. There would be almost no escape, especially with four people inhabiting one dorm suite, usually mocking each other. Whereas other students were looking forward to that new milieu, Andrew was dreading the experience.

However, things turned out to be not as bad as he had anticipated. Soon after he arrived, Andrew met a professor in mathematics with whom he could easily communicate. Together with him, he could finally develop strategies to solve a problem that had long occupied his mind. The classes were easy, no problem for him, and he stayed away from all the usual social gatherings to which freshmen typically flock. Hence it seemed that Andrew had found some peace of mind in his little niche in mathematics, where he could withdraw and pursue his interests. College life did not matter for him, only mathematics.

Outbreak of Schizophrenic Symptoms

Toward the end of the first year, however, things changed. Now Andrew was forced to take various examinations in the different fields. This was no problem for him in math and physics, obviously, but the humanities proved to be obstinate and rather difficult for him to understand. Worst of all, he was approached by a girl for the first time in his life. Though attracted to girls, he never really knew how to approach them, made even more complicated by his socially awkward behavior: The closer people came to him, the more anxious he got. He fantasized about all kinds of difficulties and how to respond to them—what would be appropriate for him to say. As easy as mathematics and its logical reasoning came to him, social interaction, which required the feeling and understanding the other person's mind, was much harder. He often reasoned for hours and days about how to react and reply to other people. What we usually do automatically and do not even think about was, for Andrew, a matter of long, dwindling thoughts and strategies.

When Laura, another college freshman in mathematics, approached him, these thoughts occupied his mind more and more. Whereas he had initially enjoyed seeing her in the math classes and exchanging mathematical formulas with her, he now dreaded the idea even of seeing her from a distance, let alone meeting her in the classroom. How to avoid her? The only way was to stay away from the classes by staying home, which is exactly what he did. He became even more socially isolated than before.

Staying at home did him no good, though. His perceptions started to change. He perceived things more intensely; the colors became shinier, more vivid. The red of the brick buildings on the Harvard campus became so intense that it felt as though it were poking him in his eyes. Worst of all, sounds became so intense that he started wearing earplugs all the time. Instead of becoming calmer, as he usually did when withdrawing socially, he now became more excited and aroused. *Something strange is happening*, he thought to himself.

The feeling only worsened. When out shopping, he noticed that people around him were sending messages. When they looked at him, they told him to leave Cambridge. Though not saying this verbally, he could see it in their eyes and the ways he reacted to them. Once he saw Laura who, in the way she twinkled her eyes, clearly conveyed the message that he, Andrew, must leave Cambridge to save the world by teaching mathematics. Laura also started speaking to him even when she was not physically present, telling him that he should go to New York City. Following her advice, he left Cambridge on a bus for New York City.

Acute Schizophrenic Symptoms

Arriving in the Chinatown section of New York City, he immediately looked for a spot in a park where he could settle down. The people here were also sending messages to him that he needed to save the world by teaching and spreading mathematics. That is exactly what he did. He bought big paper walls and pencils, and began writing mathematical formulas on them and teaching them to anyone he saw. He talked to passersby on the street, pulling them toward his paper walls and their mathematical formulas. After having done this for a couple of days, his perceptions further intensified and his thoughts raced through his mind. But the thoughts were continuously interrupted; he stopped being able to think clearly and coherently. Even doing his beloved subject, mathematics, became impossible. He could no longer develop any formulas. His mind was nothing but chaos, swirling with all kinds of different thoughts.

Andrew also noticed that a companion living in the same park had started inserting his thoughts into Andrew's mind. Andrew began to think his thoughts were no longer his own but those of his companion. How to escape all that chaos? He became increasingly certain that he was no longer himself but another person. Who was he? Why, he was the son of Albert Einstein, the brilliant physicist! When looking into a mirror at a public washroom, he noticed that he looked almost exactly like the young Albert Einstein. The only way for that to be possible, he thought, was that he, originally named Andrew, must really be the son of Albert Einstein. Therefore, when one of the park's other inhabitants asked him who he was, he responded by referring himself to as the son of Albert Einstein.

This other inhabitant became suspicious about what seemed to be Andrew's total mental confusion and decided to invite Andrew for lunch. Though he was inclined to reject the kind offer, the former Andrew, now Albert Einstein's son, was rather hungry, as he had run out of money and could not decline the friendly offer. He saw it as another opportunity to teach his host mathematics. This turned out to be impossible, though, since he was barely able to formulate any clear thoughts. Instead, his host asked him all kinds of strange questions and offered to bring him to a proper accommodation. That turned out to be the emergency room of a psychiatric hospital, where, after some considerable resistance, Andrew finally agreed to be admitted: not for treatment, though, at least in his eyes, but for accommodation and food so that he could clear his mind and continue teaching mathematics to the rest of the world.

Social Disconnection and World-Brain Disruption

What is wrong with Andrew? Something basic changed, which led him to experience himself, other selves, and the world as a whole in a completely different way. I would suggest that his relation to the world is different and, more specifically, disrupted. His world–brain relation is disrupted. His brain no longer relates him to the world in the usual way, with reciprocal balance between internal and external inputs from body and world. Instead, internal and external inputs from all three—brain, body, and world—seem to get mixed and confused. How is that possible? Andrew's brain now seems unable to establish "normal" relations with the world. What is the evidence of the change in Andrew's brain? To answer this question, we need to understand the disorder that is schizophrenia.

What is schizophrenia? The definition of schizophrenia and what causes it remain elusive. What is clear, though, are its various symptoms. Many of the most typical symptoms are illustrated in the imaginary story of Andrew. Social withdrawal at a young age is typical; many (though not all) patients with schizophrenia were loners in their childhood, preferring to play alone rather than mingling with others. Some theories in current neuroscience argue that early changes took place in these patients: birth defects, viruses at birth or soon after, the mother's older age at birth, the social environment, and many other factors have all been cited as underlying contributors to the often subtle changes in a young child's social behavior.

Another contributing factor is genetic. Recall that there was one distant uncle in Andrew's family who apparently ended up in psychiatric hospitals; often there is a "positive family history for schizophrenia," as the psychiatrists say, meaning that there is a first- or second-degree relative who suffered from schizophrenia or another serious psychiatric disorder. However, the genetic origin is not clear. Many studies have been conducted but have not established a clear genetic marker for schizophrenia. As in all other domains of psychological and neurobiological research in schizophrenia, there are multiple and often subtle changes in the genetic patterns, but no clear genetic marker yet identified.

The exacerbation of the symptoms of schizophrenia in circumstances of increased social stress is also typical. We saw that Andrew developed his symptoms when the social stress increased, as subjectively perceived; this happened when Laura approached him outside the comfortable context of math classes. Being unable to cope with such social stress, the patient withdrew even further and developed increasingly disturbing symptoms. Ralph Hoffman, a psychiatrist in New York, speaks of what he describes as "social deafferentation" (Hoffman, 2007). The patients withdraw and disconnect or *deafferentiate* (i.e., they no longer receive signals) from their social environment—which, in turn, lets them focus on their inward mental life with no external validation. This leads to an extreme imbalance between internal and external mental contents: The internal contents predominate completely, taking over in such a way that they develop "a life of their own" as they become manifest in the rather bizarre symptoms.

This description clearly provides evidence of an altered relation to the world. Schizophrenia is characterized by social disconnection; the "normal" relation to the world is disrupted. How can we better address this disorder? We, as healthy people, take the world and our relation to it for granted. All our perceptions, actions, and cognitions are based on the presupposition of such a relationship to, and integration within, the world. The basis of this presupposition involves a dose of common sense. For instance, when someone is nodding his or her head during a discussion, we (at least in the Western world) take it for granted that that person agrees with us. We sense and know this in an implicit way and presuppose a shared meaning (and agreement with the other) in our subsequent perceptions and actions. That presumption, however, is possible only on the basis of a most basic and fundamental relationship to the world that integrates us and allows us to be part of that very same world.

This integration within the world, the world–brain relation, is altered, disrupted, and ultimately lost in schizophrenia. As we can see in the case of Andrew, there is often some strange behavior observable even in childhood. For him, it is no longer evident that the nodding in a discussion means approval. It becomes questionable. He does not know what it means; he cannot take it for granted, as we do. Fittingly, the Italian psychiatrist Stanghellini speaks of a "loss of common sense" in schizophrenia (Stanghellini et al., 2015; Stanghellini & Rosfort, 2015). What is called *loss of common sense* and *social disconnection* reflects what I describe as disruption of the world–brain relation. Why and how are there such disruptions of world–brain relations? This is the focus of the following section.

Sensory Overload and World–Brain Boundaries

Another typical feature of schizophrenia is its outbreak around the ages of 18–25 years, in young adulthood, as we observed in Andrew. Why then? Nobody really knows. The brain undergoes massive reorganization in adolescence, between the ages of 14 and 18. In that time the various circuits and neural networks are newly organized and undergo major changes. Neural activity is constituted by the balance between neural excitation and inhibition. Special neurons, called *pyramidal* neurons, and their main biochemical substance, glutamate, allow for neural excitation. These neurons are tightly linked to other neurons, interneurons, and their biochemical substance GABA (gamma aminobutyric acid), which mediate neural inhibition. The neural activity we observe results from the interplay and balance between neural excitation and inhibition, that is, between glutamate and GABA. Especially GABA and the various interneurons seem to undergo massive reorganization in adolescence. Although findings in individuals who later developed schizophrenia show abnormalities in the interneurons and GABA during adolescence, their relationship to the symptoms and the disease remain unclear at this point.

GABA and its interneurons seem to be of major importance in schizophrenia, nonetheless. Many studies by the U.S. psychiatrist David Lewis (2014) reported that the dorsolateral prefrontal cortex has reduced GABA and altered interneurons in individuals with schizophrenia. There seems to be a deficit in neural inhibition, which apparently is related to alterations in GABA. Such reduced GABAergic inhibition is also assumed to be relevant in the sensory system, especially the sensory cortex. We recall that Andrew initially, when in Cambridge, suffered from an increased intensity in his auditory and visual perceptions. He saw colors more intensely, especially the color red, and he heard sounds and noise in a much more acute way.

Dan Jarvitt, a psychiatrist in New York, observed reduced

inhibition in sensory processing in the auditory and visual cortices in children who later developed schizophrenia (Javitt & Freedman, 2015). Usually, auditory and visual cortices gate and control the incoming information by inhibiting it if there is too much input at the same time. These filtering mechanisms seem to be deficient in individuals with schizophrenia: They can no longer filter and gate the incoming inputs and are easily flooded with sensory information. On an experiential level, this may be related to the experience of increased intensity in auditory and visual perceptions, as described in Andrew's case.

With too much sensory stimuli, the brain cannot filter and select the input anymore. Imagine a city like New York, which is located directly on the waterfront. Several dams and walls were built to protect the city against the water. Selected canals channel the water from the ocean in a controlled way through the city in such way that the latter remains undamaged. Now imagine that all the walls, canals, and protections break down. What would happen? The city would be flooded by water such that the distinction between city and ocean might even become blurred, if not obliterated. That is exactly the case in schizophrenia. The patient with schizophrenia is flooded by inputs from the environment. His or her brain can no longer channel the different inputs and structure and organize them accordingly.

This flooding was clearly Andrew's experience, and it occurred when he had to start taking the humanities classes and was approached by Laura. That was simply too much for him and led to the ultimate breakdown of his channels: the sensory filtering mechanisms of his brain. The distinction between inside and outside, between brain, body, and environment became blurred, if not obliterated. Andrew had entered the acute phase of his disorder.

What does Andrew's experience tell us about the world–brain relation? It tells us that the world–brain relation also includes boundaries, the selecting and filtering of events in the environment. These world-brain boundaries are apparently central in protecting the resting state of the brain and the respective person from overflow. The brain's intrinsic activity structures and organizes the continuous input from the world in spatial and temporal terms and thereby erects boundaries between world and brain: world–brain boundaries.

Delusions, Voices, and Novel Identity as the Restoration of the World–Brain Relation

After the typical initial change in perception, patients with schizophrenia often develop the commonly reported symptoms. Andrew, for instance, developed what psychiatrists call *delusions*; patients who experience delusions attribute abnormal meanings to the behaviors of other people in their environment. We recall that Andrew decoded hidden messages in the eyes of other people telling him that he had to leave Cambridge and teach mathematics. Often just a raise of the eyebrow or some other small gesture from another person is sufficient to induce such abnormal attributions in a person with schizophrenia.

The delusions are usually negative and persecutory, causing much suffering in these patients. Andrew's experience was a positive case, given that teaching mathematics was something close to his heart and part of his self and biography. Though often bizarre, the content of the delusions can relate to the person this way. The delusions may also be seen as a reaction, a compensatory strategy by means of which the patient with schizophrenia tries to make sense of his abnormal perceptions and thoughts.

Another typical symptom of schizophrenia is hallucinations, especially auditory ones. Andrew experienced those when he heard Laura's voice. As in his case, the voice often conveys messages, like going to New York, which the patients feel compelled to follow. If the patients do not follow the "advice" of their voices, the voices can become violent, threatening to impose "their will," which makes it even more painful and difficult for patients to differentiate what is real from what is illusionary.

How does the brain produce these voices? Extensive imaging studies have demonstrated that the resting-state activity in the auditory cortex is abnormally high in patients with schizophrenia (for overviews, see Ford et al., 2014; Northoff, 2014a and c). Even when they do not hear a voice in the external environment, their auditory cortical resting-state activity is abnormally high. This is especially the case when they hear an internal voice, an auditory hallucination. Most interesting, when exposed to an external sound, these patients can no longer down-modulate their abnormally increased resting-state activity in the auditory cortex. That means that the external sound leads to decreased stimulus-induced activity in the auditory cortex. The internally generated resting state activity and its internal sounds, the auditory hallucinations, dominate over the external sounds and their stimulus-induced activity. The internal–external balance in the auditory cortex is shifted more toward the internal pole at the expense of the external stimuli.

Why, though, does the abnormally high resting-state activity lead to the induction of voices? The resting-state activity could be high without leading to any voices. The answer is not clear yet. One assumption in this regard is that there are continuous changes, called *variability*, even in the resting-state activity. The abnormally high level of resting-state activity may now be accompanied by high degrees of variability, meaning that the level of auditory resting-state activity may suddenly change, for instance, from low to high. That degree of change in the resting-state activity may now be as high as the degree of change an external stimulus normally induces. If the same degree of change in activity level occurs, the perception of a voice may be induced in the resting state in the same way it is usually induced by an external voice. Future investigations will show whether this possibility is correct.

Andrew showed still other typical symptoms of schizophrenia. His thoughts were completely confused, chaotic, and racing. He remained unable to order and structure them in a proper way, as is the case for most patients with schizophrenia. Psychiatrists therefore classify schizophrenia as a *thought disorder*. Often patients can no longer concentrate. Their thoughts seem to be interrupted and fragmented, resulting in thought blockades, and there is often an overwhelming abundance of thoughts, as Andrew experienced.

Finally, Andrew took on the identity of another person, the son of Albert Einstein. That is called *ego* or *identity disturbance* by psychiatrists. This is indeed one of the most bizarre symptoms of schizophrenia. Patients experience themselves as another person, as another person's *self*. They often take on the identity of a famous person such as Jesus, Buddha, Nefertiti, or the president or head-of-state of their country. Why that is so remains unclear, but this (unconscious) choice of esteemed or revered identity delves deeply into the issue of the sense of self, and its underlying neural mechanisms, which characterizes human experience. What is wrong in the brain of patients with schizophrenia who experience themselves as another person? This question is closely related to the question of the basic disturbance in schizophrenia, which is discussed in the next section.

First, however, let's consider the relevance of these symptoms for my concept of the world–brain relation. Symptoms such as delusions and identity change can be regarded as the reaction to a disruption in the boundaries between world and brain; the boundaries between world and brain become blurred and ultimately break down. Consequently patients become confused about *what is world* and *what is self*, what is inside and what is outside. In my view, the schizophrenic symptoms can be seen as attempt to reorganize the self and its relation to the world. They are a compensatory strategy to rebuild what is lost or disrupted in the world–brain relation.

Basic Disturbance and Estrangement of the Self from the World

Where do these bizarre symptoms come from and what is their underlying cause? At the beginning of the 20th century, when brain imaging had not yet been developed, psychiatrists in Germany and Switzerland, such as Emil Kraepelin and Eugen Bleuler, having nothing to rely on but clinical observation, assumed abnormality of the self to be basic and fundamental in schizophrenia. (As we will see later, neuroimaging has revealed the neural basis of the basic disturbance in the schizophrenic brain.) Kraeplin characterized schizophrenia as "the peculiar destruction of the inner coherence of the personality" with a "disunity of consciousness" ("orchestra without conductor") (1913, p. 668). Bleuler also pointed out that schizophrenia is a "disorder of the personality by splitting, dissociation" where the "I is never completely intact" (1911, p. 58).

A German contemporary of Bleuler and Kraepelin, Josef Berze (1914) even referred to schizophrenia as a "basic alteration of self-consciousness." Another famous German psychiatrist, Karl Jaspers, also noticed "incoherence, dissociation, fragmenting of consciousness, intrapsychic ataxia, weakness of apperception, insufficiency of psychic activity and disturbance of association" to be the unifying "central factor" in schizophrenia (1964/1997, p. 581).

How is such basic disturbance of the self manifested in patients' subjective experience of their own selves? The earlier descriptions of a disrupted self are complemented by current phenomenological accounts that focus predominantly on the experience of oneself in relation to the world. Josef Parnas, a Danish psychiatrist, well describes how "presence" is altered in schizophrenia (2003; Parnas et al., 2001). The experience of the world and its objects are no longer accompanied by a prereflective self-awareness. That is, the self that experiences the world is no longer included in that very experience:

> The prominent feature of altered presence in the pre-onset stages of schizophrenia is disturbed ipseity, a disturbance in which the sense of self no longer saturates the

experience. For instance, the sense of mineness of experience may become subtly affected: one of our patients reported that this feeling of his experience as his own experience only "appeared a split-second delayed." (Parnas, 2003, p. 225)

The patients are unable to refer to themselves in their experience of the world. It is as if the experience of the world is no longer *their* experience. Because their very sense of self is absent in their experience of the world, patients with schizophrenia become detached, alienated, and estranged from that very experience. This detachment from their own selfhood makes it impossible for them to feel their experiences as subjective. The experiencing self is consequently no longer affected by its own experiences, which Sass (2003) describes as a "disorder of self-affectivity": The self is no longer experienced as one's own and, most importantly, is no longer felt as the vital center and source of experience, actions, perceptions, thoughts. This state reflects what Sass (2003) calls "diminished self-affection," meaning that the self is no longer affected by its own experiences.

If the self is no longer affected by its own experience, then the self stands apart from the objects and the events in the world that are experienced. A gulf, a phenomenological distance, as Parnas says (2003, p. 225), opens up between the world and the self. The objects and events of the world no longer intuitively make sense and are thus no longer meaningful to the experiencing subject. One's own self becomes almost objective and mechanical in its experience and perception of the world.

More generally, the self becomes alienated from the

world. The self experiences itself as no longer part of the world; there is a distance between world and self, which, as I assume, can be traced back to world–brain disruption. Where does this world–brain disruption come from? What is altered in the brain in schizophrenia? These questions lead us back to the resting state and the midline regions in the brain.

Disruption in the Brain and the Missing Rest–Stimulus Interaction

Recall from Chapter 3 that self-specific stimuli were specifically associated with neural activity changes in the cortical midline structures, the regions in the midline of the brain. Interestingly, these regions also show extremely high levels of neural activity in the resting state, during the absence of specific tasks or stimuli. Most importantly, the high levels of resting-state activity in these regions seem to overlap with, and predict, the neural activity changes during self-specific stimuli.

Taken together, these findings suggest a close relationship between the intrinsic activity in the midline brain regions and the sense of self or self-specificity. The intrinsic activity may then be supposed to contain, encode, and ingrain some information about the self and its self-specificity. If so, one would now expect the abnormalities of self in schizophrenia to be characterized by abnormalities in both resting-state and stimulus-induced activity during self-specific stimuli. This is exactly what the research findings suggest.

Various studies have investigated the midline regions

of the brain as part of the default-mode network (DMN) in schizophrenia. Imaging studies in schizophrenia reported abnormal resting-state activity and functional connectivity, especially in the anterior cortical midline structures (aCMS). One study (Whitfield-Gabrieli et al., 2009) demonstrated that the aCMS and the posterior CMS, such as the posterior cingulate cortex (PCC) and precuneus, no longer show as much activity change in response to short-term memory tasks. This finding suggests that the resting state is no longer as reactive to stimuli; the resting state does not respond to extrinsic stimuli and can therefore no longer induce proper activity changes in response to cognitive tasks. This decreased activity change was observed in both patients with schizophrenia and their relatives when compared to healthy individuals.

Furthermore, the very same patients also showed increased functional connectivity—that is, temporal synchronization across different regions—of the aCMS with other posterior regions of the CMS, the PCC. This suggests that the regions were very tightly coupled with each other and, as noted, closely synchronized temporally with each other. Most interestingly, the degree of functional hyperconnectivity correlated with the positive symptoms of schizophrenia, such as auditory hallucinations and delusions, in these patients: the higher the degree of functional hyperconnectivity in the CMS, the stronger the positive symptoms of delusions and hallucinations.

Decreased activity changes in the aCMS were also observed in a study that likewise investigated working memory (Pomarol-Clotet et al., 2008). Similar to the study described above, these researchers asked participants to perform a working memory task. The researchers observed abnormally decreased activity changes in the aCMS in patients with schizophrenia, compared to healthy individuals. Similar to other investigators, the researchers also observed abnormal task-related activation in the right dorsolateral prefrontal cortex in patients with schizophrenia. Other studies (for an overview, see Northoff, 2015b) also reported abnormal activity changes in the aCMS, as well as abnormal functional connectivity in these patients from the aCMS and posterior CMS to the insula.

In addition to the task-induced deactivation and abnormal functional connectivity seen in patients with schizophrenia, another abnormal measure of resting-state activity has been reported—specifically, fluctuations or oscillations in certain temporal frequencies. For example, Hoptman and colleagues (Hoptman et al., 2010) demonstrated that low-frequency fluctuations in the resting state were increased in the aCMS (and in the parahippocampal gyrus) in patients with schizophrenia. In contrast, other regions such as the insula showed decreased low-frequency fluctuations. Abnormally increased low-frequency oscillations (< 0.06 Hz) in the aCMS (and posterior CMS regions and the auditory network) and their correlation with positive symptom severity were also observed in another study on patients with schizophrenia.

What do these research findings mean? The low-frequency fluctuations show extremely long cycle durations. These long cycle durations link and integrate different stimuli and events that, in healthy people, are usually processed in a segregated way. Is this the mechanism that allows the patient with schizophrenia to link events that are disconnected in the "real world," such as the shaking of his or her head and the bending of the tree by the wind? For the patient it is his or her head shaking that causes the wind to bend the tree; for the psychiatrist, such thinking is a delusion.

The findings from these studies on the resting state suggest that the spatial and temporal structure of the resting state is abnormal in schizophrenia. The spatial structure, as indexed by functional connectivity, is abnormally tight and can therefore no longer change in response to extrinsic stimuli. The temporal structure, as established by the frequency fluctuations, is also abnormal and seems to exhibit too much power in especially the long, slow cycle durations. That abnormality in frequency fluctuations in turn leads the patient with schizophrenia to integrate and link stimuli that usually do not belong together. It is clear from this research base that the spatial and temporal abnormalities in the resting state strongly impact the brain's reaction to external stimuli especially from the environment (and also to internal stimuli from the body).

The resting state no longer seems to allow for proper interface with extrinsic stimuli—that is, for an optimal rest–stimulus interaction. More generally, the brain can no longer interact with the world; the world–brain relation, as indexed by rest–stimulus interaction, is disrupted such that the brain and its resting state are no longer updated and modulated by the world and its various inputs. Indeed, there is *no* rest–stimulus interaction anymore. The brain and its resting state consequently lose their connection to the world and process and change their activity independently of what is going on in the world. The world–brain relation is absent as the schizophrenic symptoms become present.

The Self in Schizophrenia and the Mismatching between World and Rest

In addition to its resting-state activity, the brain can also be characterized by stimulus-induced activity known as *extrinsic stimuli*. As we saw in Chapter 3, one can use self-specific stimuli (e.g., one's name) to investigate how they impact neural activity in the brain. Comparisons can then be made between their effects and those of non-self-specific stimuli (e.g., another person's name).

This experiment typically has been performed with healthy people, but some studies have used patients with schizophrenia as participants. An imaging study by Holt and colleagues (Holt et al., 2011) showed that abnormal anterior-to-posterior midline connectivity is related to self-specificity processing in patients with schizophrenia. These researchers investigated the performance of patients with schizophrenia during a word task, wherein people had to judge trait adjectives according to their degree of self-specificity, and during two other tasks: one involving other reflection (i.e., relation of a displayed word to another person) and perception reflection (i.e., words printed in upper- or lowercase letters).

What did the results show? Patients with schizophrenia demonstrated significantly elevated activity in posterior midline regions such as the mid- and posterior cingulate cortex during self-reflection on the trait adjective task. Meanwhile, signal changes in the anterior midline regions, such as the medial prefrontal cortex, were significantly reduced when compared to healthy individuals. Finally, functional connectivity was abnormally elevated from the posterior to the anterior midline regions in patients with schizophrenia. Analogous results of altered midline activity with an altered relationship—that is, imbalance between anterior and posterior midline regions—were also observed in other studies on self-specificity in schizophrenia.

Taken together, these results demonstrate that patients with schizophrenia have abnormal resting-state activity, especially in the midline regions that are involved in processing self-related stimuli. The very same network also shows alterations in the balance between anterior and posterior midline regions when probing for self-specific stimuli.

Now we can raise the question of whether these abnormalities in stimulus-induced activity are related to the resting-state abnormalities. Unfortunately, at this time, studies testing the linkage between resting-state abnormalities and self-specific stimuli still need to be conducted on patients with schizophrenia. These results are needed in order to support the assumption that the information about the self that is contained within the intrinsic activity of the brain may serve as a measure for the assignment of self-specificity to extrinsic stimuli. To put it differently, the resting-state abnormalities may signify what earlier psychiatrists described as the basic disturbance of the self observed in patients with schizophrenia. Meanwhile, the stimulus-induced activity changes that are associated with self-specific stimuli may correspond to the abnormal subjective experience of the self, as described by Parnas and other contemporary psychiatrists.

Furthermore, such resting-state-based disturbance of

the self also disrupts the relation of the resting state to the environment: the world–brain relation. The self provides the structure and organization to establish relation to the world; this self-specific structure and organization are encoded in yet unclear ways in the spatial–temporal organization of the resting state (see Chapter 3). The spatial–temporal structure of the resting state links the extrinsic stimuli from the environment to the brain; this is most likely accomplished by matching the spatial–temporal structure of the extrinsic stimuli—the sequence of their occurrence in time and space within the environment—with the one in the brain's resting state (see Northoff, 2014b). The better the spatial–temporal structure of the stimuli from the environment match the one in the resting-state activity, the higher the degree of self-specificity or self-relatedness is assigned to the former.

This mutual matching process between the spatial–temporal structures of extrinsic stimuli and the resting state seems to no longer operate in schizophrenia. Why and how is unclear at this point in time. What *is* clear is that the mismatching disrupts the world–brain relation, which makes these patients unable to assign any degree of self-specificity or self-relatedness to events in the environment. If there is no self-specificity or self-relatedness anymore, everything in the world appears as strange and bizarre, as was the case for Andrew in New York. In order to make sense of the events in the world, Andrew came up with explanations that are as bizarre to us with our healthy minds as the world was for him on the basis of his unwell brain. We call Andrew's state *delusional*, whereas from his point of view, he was simply developing a view and explanation of the world that was coherent for him.

Schizophrenia: A Spatial–Temporal Disorder of the Resting State of the Brain?

So, what is schizophrenia? We currently do not know. Though several neuronal abnormalities have been reported, we currently have no idea of the neuronal mechanisms accounting for these abnormalities or for the various symptoms. Therefore, we currently lack diagnostic and therapeutic markers, as well as proper and specific treatment. What *can* we learn from this chapter, given all the negatives I just stated? Schizophrenia may be a disorder of the resting state and its spatial and temporal structures. If that is the case, we would expect the various symptoms in schizophrenia to be primarily spatial–temporal symptoms of the abnormalities in the resting-state activity, rather than being sensorimotor, affective, cognitive, or social symptoms of the brain's stimulus-induced activity (for instance, see Northoff, 2015a and b, see Northoff in press-a; in press-b for an analogous spatiotemporal account of psychopathological symptoms in depression).

This is a rather bold assumption on my part at this point in time. Why? We neither understand the resting state of the brain, by itself, let alone the kind of spatial–temporal structures it apparently constructs. Once we understand both of these areas better, we may have an opportunity to view schizophrenic symptoms in a spatial–temporal context. We would then need to characterize the various symptoms in spatial–temporal terms and relate them to specific spatial–temporal features in the brain's resting-state activity. This endeavour could be called a *spatial–temporal approach* to psychiatric disorders such as schizophrenia.

Such an approach would not only allow a deeper and

better understanding of schizophrenic symptoms but also offer novel treatment options. We could then aim to develop strategies to specifically modulate the spatial–temporal structure of the resting state by applying spatially and temporally modulating stimuli. This could be done, for instance, with music stimuli in the form of music therapy—though in a more targeted and neurophysiologically (i.e., resting-state-based) way—as well as by novel drugs or other tools (e.g., magnetic stimulation) that modulate specific spatial or temporal features of the resting-state activity. If such spatial–temporal therapy were effective, it would offer novel treatment options for patients with schizophrenia.

At the same time, spatial–temporal therapy approaches would tell us whether our assumption about the central role of the spatial–temporal structure in the resting state in mediating neural–mental transformation is right or wrong. If the supposed spatial–temporal therapy works, we must be somehow right. If, in contrast, it does not help alleviate these patients' symptoms, we would conclude that this mechanism may have no role in neural–mental transformation. The future holds the answer, but only after extensive neuroscientific, psychiatric, and neurophilosophical investigations.

What Schizophrenia Can Tell Us about Our Existence in the World

Schizophrenia can tell us not only about neural–mental transformation but also about the deepest and most basic layers of our existence. The disruption of the world–brain relation that occurs in schizophrenia leads to disastrous consequences that change everything, including the most basic sense of self. If the most fundamental world–brain relation is disrupted, basic human certainties are cast into doubt and we lose our anchor in the world. We are then no longer part of this world, which itself then becomes questionable, and, as in delusions, nothing but a dangerous and threatening place. Every understanding of others, our common sense or invisible bond with other persons and their mental states, is lost. The patient with schizophrenia is locked into his or her own brain, decoupled and detached from the rest of the world. That, as we have seen in the case of Andrew, threatens the whole existence. Schizophrenia can therefore be conceived as an existential disorder in the same way the world–brain relation can be described as an existential relation.

There is much at stake when we flesh out the world–brain relation. In neuroscientific terms, the exact neural mechanisms of how the brain and its resting state link themselves and integrate within the world, in the world–brain relation, remain to be explored in detail (see chapter 20 in Northoff, 2014c for details about what I there describe as environment-brain unity). We have seen that abnormal psychiatric shifts in the world–brain relation lead to depression (see Chapter 4) whereas its disruption causes the more severe psychiatric disorder of schizophrenia.

In philosophy the world–brain relation is essential for mental features such as consciousness and self, so the mind–brain problem must be reformulated as world–brain problem. The world–brain relation makes it clear that *there is no mind*. If the mind does not exist, there is also no need to discuss its potential relationship to the brain, even if one assumes the mind to be the brain. One should better focus on the overlap and shared features between world and brain,

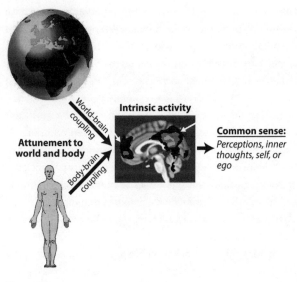

Figure 6.1a

the world–brain relation, and how that interface in turn predisposes mental features such as consciousness and self.

Finally, in addition to its metaphysical relevance for mental features, the world–brain relation also carries major existential implications. Our existence is deeply rooted in and based on the world–brain relation, the continuous matching and adaptation of the brain's resting state to its respective environmental context. Only on the basis of this world–brain relation can we experience ourselves as part of the world and capable of developing a sense of self (as it is lost, for instance, in schizophrenia).

The world–brain relation signifies our existence and the sense of self we each possess; without it, we experience loss of both existence and of self, as is observed in

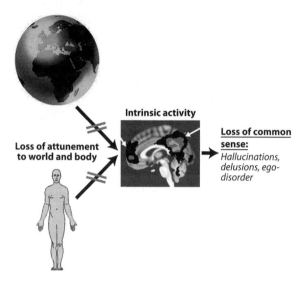

Figure 6.1b

schizophrenia. We, and that sense of self we each embody, *are* the world–brain relation. That is all there is. That is our existence—an existence that is intrinsically relational and therefore anchored in the world. There is nothing else apart from such relational existence and its world–brain relation.

The world–brain relation demarcates the boundaries not only of our existence but also of philosophy in general. Beyond that we can do nothing but speculate and assume illusory entities such as a mind. We are then becoming delusional about a world outside and beyond our own world in more or less the same way. Andrew and other patients with schizophrenia are delusional with respect to the world in which they actually live and share with us.

Chapter 7

IDENTITY AND TIME

==== **PREVIEW** ====
How is the world–brain relation constituted?

I have assumed the central role of the world–brain relation in emotional feeling and its disruption in schizophrenia and depression. These disorders demonstrate clearly that the world–brain relation is central for mental features such as sense of self, and even more basic for our existence as part of this world. That line of thinking, though, leaves unaddressed the question of how the world–brain relation is constituted. What is the mechanism upon which the world–brain is established? Let's return to a consideration of schizophrenia. We saw in Andrew, our case example, that he suffered from a change in his identity when experiencing himself as another person. This fundamental change leads us to ponder what philosophically is described as *personal identity*: the identification or persistence of one's own sense of personhood as one and the same across time. The relationship between *personal identity* and *time* and how it constitutes the world-brain relation is the focus in this final chapter.

Discontinuity of World and Brain versus Continuity of Self and Identity

We focus again on Andrew from the previous chapter and his experience as a different person because of schizophrenia, what psychiatrists call *identity disturbance*. Did Andrew lose his identity? Was he no longer the same person? Or was it just a mental illusion such that we can therefore consider him to have remained the same person with the same identity throughout the psychotic episode? Andrew's case raises questions about what constitutes personal identity and how we can define it.

Humans are exposed to time, which changes us and perennially continues. We get older and our outlook changes; our skin wrinkles, our muscles weaken. Despite all the physical changes in our body, however, we still experience ourselves as the same person. I am now the same person as the one who, 20 years ago, fell in love for the first time. Although my body has changed continuously, I nevertheless remain one and the same person in my conscious experience of myself. How is that possible? This problem has been discussed in philosophy as the question of personal identity, with this concept describing the identity of a person across time.

The relationship between identity and time presents us with a paradox. On the one hand, we are subject to time and its continuous flow. Everything changes in us and around us: our bodies, our environments, our thoughts—the contents in our consciousness flow continuously from one to another. Neuroscientists discovered that even the brain itself and its resting-state activity are never the same. There is continuous change, which is indexed by what is called *variability.* The amplitude of the resting-state activity continuously changes, which can be measured by calculating the variance, or variability. Variability with change across time is important. We saw, for instance, that too strong a decrease in resting-state variability in the midline regions leads to the loss of consciousness, as in vegetative state (see Chapters 1 and 2). If there is no variability whatsoever in the brain's resting-state activity, the person will slip into coma and ultimately become brain-dead, in which every neural activity ceases.

Even the cells, the neurons of the brain, change continuously; they are unceasingly produced, such that the neurons that sustain my resting state now are no longer the same as the ones from 20 years ago. This ongoing state of change is what neuroscientists call *plasticity.* Plasticity is present on all levels of the brain, from the resting-state activity to the neurons and the regions, the networks and the circuits that all continuously change in their level and extent of structure and activity.

So, given that the brain is variable and flexible and undergoes continuous change, how is it possible that our sense of self and its subsequent personal identity remain the same? My brain and its resting-state activity change during the night when I sleep. However, I nevertheless wake up the next morning with an experience of my self as the same self who went to sleep the night before. My personal identity is preserved. Despite all the change in my brain, my self and its identity are the same. Change in brain; no change in identity. How is that possible?

Are self and its personal identity *not* based on brain activity but on something else that does not undergo continuous change, instead remaining essentially the same across time? In order to address this question, we need to search for the features that remain continuous over time. And again, we learn from schizophrenia. Andrew and other patients with schizophrenia experience a change in their identities; they are now different persons. The continuous change in the resting-state activity of their brains apparently no longer performs the neural–mental transformations in a way that preserves their selves and their identities. The discontinuity of the brain no longer leads to continuity but to discontinuity of self. How is that possible? That question is the focus of the following section.

Diachronic and Synchronic Identity

What accounts for such continuity over time? Is it our bodies, our memories, or something we could think of as the mind? These are the kind of questions raised when discussing the concept of personal identity. It is not a homogeneous concept but rather a mixed bag of heterogeneous problems. One problem is already embedded in the concept of *personal*. What makes someone a person rather than some mere object? How can we define the notion of person? This has been called the *question of personhood*.

One possible approach to the question of personhood is the characterization of ourselves as matter. Are we nothing but mere physical matter, just body and brain? Are we just human animals, as Eric Olson (1997) says? This premise would make it problematic to distinguish humans from nonhumans. Other authors argue for us being only a bundle of perceptions, as can be traced back to the Scottish philosopher David Hume. There is also the question of whether we, as persons, are specific metaphysical entities or substances, as, for instance, a physical or mental entity. The quest for the basic metaphysical characterization is raised.

The central issue in the concept of personal identity concerns the second term *identity*. What makes a person identical through the passage of time? Am I, at age 52, still the same person I was at 23? A person certainly undergoes major changes throughout the passage of time, from physical changes like the wrinkling of skin and the greying of hair, to mental changes in thoughts, beliefs, and attitudes. But despite all these mental and physical changes, I am still the same person. What are the conditions underlying continuity of identity as a particular person over time?

The question regarding the temporal continuity of identity can also be called the question of *persistence* or *diachronic identity*—and diachronic identity can be discussed in terms of different criteria, such as *identity through time*. The body persists through time, and though it undergoes major changes, it still remains one and the same body so that we may assume what is called *physical continuity*. Or one may want to argue that the psychological functions remain the same, providing *psychological continuity*. One psychological function particularly relevant in this context is memory, as noted initially by the British philosopher John Locke. The ability to memorize events and our selves from earlier times and recall them at a later time point may provide the temporal continuity necessary to identify our own persons as one and the same over time.

We can ask questions about the identity of a person in two different ways: What makes someone the person he or she is at one particular point in time, and what makes someone persist as the same person over time? The latter notion of diachronic identity may be complemented by the former one of synchronic identity. I may be more than one person throughout the passage of time—this possibility is raised by diachronic identity. But I may also be more than one person at one particular point in time, which is a possibility in synchronic identity. This could be the case if my brain were split into its two halves, or if I suffered from what is called *dissociative identity disorder* (more commonly known as *multiple personality disorder*), whereby different selves or persons coexist in one and the same body at the same time. Do I have two identities related to the two split halves of my brain? Where psychiatrists speak here of dissociative identity disorder, philosophers speak of personal identity, and neuroscientists just see two hemispheres. We will return to these questions later.

Memories and Identity

What accounts for our sense of identity as persons across time? Memory is one often-discussed possibility. Early philosophers such as John Locke argued that by remembering episodes from the past and attributing them to the same person, we establish continuity of that person across time. It must be one and the same person who experienced a particular event in the past and who now, in the present, remembers that very same event. The continuity that memory provides therefore accounts for our personal identity.

What do neurophilosophers have to say about identity? They would first make the philosopher aware that there are different memory systems in the brain: short-term or working memory, procedural memory, and episodic memory. Short-term memory is involved in memorizing the series of numbers you want to enter into your cell phone; this is called *working memory* and is related to particular regions in the brain, such as the prefrontal cortex. There is also the memory involved in your movements and actions. You learn complicated actions like riding bikes, playing tennis, perhaps even pole vaulting over time by training; your sensorimotor systems must have some kind of memory by which to store previous movements and actions. This is called *procedural memory* and is related to the premotor and sensorimotor cortex in the brain.

Another memory system is episodic or autobiographical memory, whereby experiences are stored. For instance, I remember that I already read this chapter yesterday. And I remember vividly that I had problems understanding what the philosophers mean by personal identity, as I sipped on my tea and my cell phone continuously showed new messages coming in. Outside it was snowing like crazy, and the temperature had fallen down to minus-40 degrees. That is the episode I remember today about my experience yesterday in Canada. My friend who just arrived today from Taiwan read the same book chapter yesterday, but he remembers it completely differently. He was lying in the sun, on the beach, in 104-degree weather, occasionally glancing at this chapter in the book beside him. Despite not being in the Canadian winter yesterday, we consider him to be the same person as when he experienced the 104-degree blazing sun on the beach.

Finally, the neurophilosopher will say that this amounts to what is meant by *personal identity*: Episodic or autobiographical memory is the basis of our personal identity, whereas working memory and procedural memory remain more or less irrelevant to that identity (whereas they may be central to the identity of dancers, athletes, and the like,

for whom movement sequences are crucial). Without episodic memory, the person's sense of identity would no longer
remain continuous across time. Hence, episodic memory is
the basis of personal identity. More specifically, the temporal continuity of persons is mediated by episodic memory
and its related neural systems in the brain, the hippocampus in the medial temporal lobe and the cortical midline
structures in the middle of the brain.

Memory and Change

Things are not so easy, however. We are all, including the
neurophilosophers, well aware that our memory can deceive
us. Consider the following example. You vividly remember
the supermarket robbery that occurred yesterday. While
you were in the supermarket in the morning looking for your
favorite yogurt, there were suddenly three men with black
masks entering the corridor, pushing all customers and per-
sonnel, including you, outside the main entrance door. Then
they closed the supermarket, went into the back, stole all
the money, and left through the back door before the police
arrived 10 minutes later. You still remember the shock and
anxiety, and even feel anxious today thinking about it.
Wasn't that you who experienced the robbery? And can it
be only you who remembers this episode, since you experienced it? You cannot remember having experienced something that you did not actually experience, can you?

The next day you read the story about the same event
in the newspaper. Was it really the same event? The article reports five rather than three men with black masks all
entering at the same time. In addition to the money, they
stole plenty of the goods. They also left the supermarket

through the front door rather than back door, where they aggressively pushed one customer aside and almost threw her to the floor. Now you recall that that is exactly what happened to you: *You* were pushed aside by one of the guys and almost tumbled to the floor, but in the last second were able to regain your balance.

However, all that is cast into doubt when you continue reading. The newspaper writes that the robbery occurred in the evening rather than morning as you recall it. Was it really the same robbery? Yes, it occurred in exactly the same supermarket you were in yesterday and the details written seem to somehow mesh with what you recall. Now you ask yourself: Did I really experience the supermarket robbery or am I deceived by own memories? Or was it a different person experiencing that robbery? Your autobiographical or episodic memory may have deceived you. This scenario clearly reveals the close relationship between memory and self.

The fact that our episodic memory can deceive us does not speak in favor of memory providing the necessary sense of continuity through time. Memory seems to be as discontinuous as world, body, and brain. Our memories change. Our childhood memories change according to the context in which we relive and re-experience them. What was painful shortly after the event is recalled later as the greatest episode in the person's life. Memories are as variable and flexible as the resting-state activity of the brain. Though the details are not fully known yet, it is clear that memories must be somehow encoded in the brain's resting-state activity. The spatial–temporal structure of resting-state activity is susceptible to life events. One of our studies (Duncan et al., in press) shows that the *degree of functional connectivity and entropy* (e.g., disorder in activity pattern) *in the resting state* is closely related to the *degree of stressful life events in the person's childhood*: The more stressful life events experienced during childhood, the stronger the functional connectivity and entropy between the amygdala, a region in charge of emotions, and the midline region that is related to our sense of self.

These findings suggest that brain's resting state encodes life events in its neural activity and stores the information. However, the continuous change in the resting state may then also affect what is encoded from previous life events and thus what can be recalled about them at later moments in time: Even the life events themselves and our memories of them do not remain 100% continuous over time. Due to their variability and continuous change, memories are not the proper candidate for preserving the identity of the person over time. The expert philosopher says that memories are not transitive: Person A remembers Person B, who in turn remembers Person C; this, though, does not imply that Person A also remembers Person C. This lack of transitiveness does not apply in the case of identity. Person A is identical to Person B, who in turn is identical to Person C; this sequence entails that Person A is also identical to Person C. In short, *identity is transitive*; memory is not. Therefore memory cannot serve as candidate for constituting personal identity. We need to look for another possible candidate that allows for continuity, rather than change, over time.

Body and Mind

Philosophers have reverted to criteria other than memory as the basis for identity for the reasons just noted. These include other psychological functions such as attention and consciousness. The psychological continuity these functions provide may then be the basis of personal identity. According to the British philosopher Derek Parfit, who wrote the philosophically well-known book *Reasons and Persons* (1984), personal identity is a matter of psychological continuity. Parfit de-emphasized the importance of personal identity, writing basically that identity does not matter; only survival matters, and survival can diverge from identity. Before going into that topic, we shall briefly discuss other criteria of personal identity.

The body can also be a criterion of personal identity. One's own body is always there and with the death of the body, the person vanishes too. Is the person and his or her identity across time thus nothing more than the body and its physical continuity? That doesn't seem to be an option either. Our bodies continuously change, as noted; our skin grows old, our organs fail, the heart gets weak and slow, and breathing becomes more difficult in old age. And even when we are young, there are continuous changes to our bodies. The body seems to provide discontinuity and change rather than continuity and sameness, so the body and its alleged physical continuity cannot really serve as the basis of a person's sense of continuity or personal identity.

One last option in which to locate this continuity may be the brain. The brain is always there; it is continuous across time, entailing neural continuity. Does the brain's neural continuity provide continuity for me as a person, for my personal identity? If so, I am my brain, whereas I am not my memory or my body. Are we really nothing but our brains? The brain is apparently central for shaping us as persons, including our personalities. But is it really the basis of our identity as persons?

Philosophers who assume the existence and reality of a mind distinct from the brain (see Chapter 4) would certainly object. Our identity as persons is provided by the mind rather than by the brain, they say, and the brain continuously changes in the same way as does the body. Due to such continuous change, the brain cannot serve as the basis of our identity as persons. Instead of either brain or body, there must be something that is continuous and remains the same across time without being subject to change. That is only possible for the mind. Our identity as persons must thus be mental rather than either psychological (as in the case of memory), physical (as in the case of the body), or neural (as in the case of the brain).

The concept of mind is here the placeholder for *nonchange*, the absence of change. Memories and bodies change and therefore do not underlie the identity of persons over time and the experience of self. Since we cannot find anything that does not change in the world we live in, we must assume something else from somewhere else that does not change. This "something else" is the mind, which must originate "somewhere else," in a world beyond the one in which we actually live. The mind is supposed to remain the same over time; it is continuous over time and shows no change and variability at all. These features can be traced back to Descartes's description of the mind as a mental substance (*res cogitans*, thinking thing), making the mind a perfect candidate to underlie identity and its continuity over time.

How about schizophrenia? Schizophrenia manifests identity disturbances such that the identity is transformed into nonidentity with the subsequent experience of a different self. There is no continuity of the self over time. At least in their subjective experience, patients with schizophrenia lose their identity and replace it with a new one. Most interestingly, the novel identity is strongly context-dependent. For instance, patients in the Western world often take on the identity of Jesus, especially if they have a strong religious background and context. In contrast, these patients in China often exchange their identity for the one of Mao Tse-tung (or Mao Zedong), the long-standing revolutionary leader during the 20th century.

If the assumption of the mind as the underlying substrate of identity were correct, one would expect schizophrenia to be a disturbance of the mind. Schizophrenia is a *mental* disorder. This has indeed been the long-held view. However, as described in the previous chapter, there are major, though not yet fully identified, alterations in the brains of patients with schizophrenia. Schizophrenia may therefore be rather a neural disorder—a disorder of the brain and how it relates to the world—than a mental disorder of the mind. This reality leads us back to the brain. Is the brain the source of personal identity and continuity over time?

The Discontinuity of the Brain over Time: "Am I My Brain or Not?"

Memory, body, brain, or mind: Which one is the basis of our identity as persons? Am I my brain? This is the central question at this point in our discussion. The American philosopher Thomas Nagel considers the brain as both a necessary and sufficient criterion for personal identity, which results in the statement "I am my brain." Nagel (1974) considers the term *identity* to be a definitive and nonconventional term. It is *definitive* in the sense that it refers to a yes-or-no, all-or-nothing decision with regard to identity. Either a person is identical or nonidentical over time. There are no intermediaries. Identity is nonconventional in the sense that it does not entail its own necessary and sufficient conditions and therefore contains an "empty position" that must be filled by an "additional fact." Nagel compares the term *identity* with that of *gold*. Before the chemical formula for gold was detected, the term *gold* contained an "empty position" that later was filled by an "additional fact" of its chemical formula.

So what might the "additional fact" that could fill the "empty position" of personal identity be? We currently do not know. Whatever it is, this additional fact needed for identity must bridge the gap between the subjective experience of the person—that is, his or her first-person perspective—and its "I," on the one hand, and the objective necessary structures—that is, its body or its existence—on the other. Since the brain might eventually bridge this gap between subjective experience and objective structures, it may be considered as a suitable candidate to fill the "empty position."

On the one hand, the brain must be considered as the necessary foundation for the possibility of subjective experience, since without the brain we remain unable to experience mental states in First-Person Perspective. On the other hand, the brain is the carrier of psychophysiological processes that are essential for regulating and maintaining the body. In contrast to other organs, like, for example, the liver or kidney, damage to the brain is often accompanied by changes in personal identity. This is true in cases of schizophrenia wherein sufferers may experience themselves as different persons, as we saw in the previous chapter. The brain must subsequently be regarded as the basis of personal identity.

How, though, is that possible? The brain shows continuous change and variability in its resting-state activity. The resting state appears to show an as yet unclear, though present, spatial and temporal structure. This spatial–temporal structure is not written in stone, so to speak. On the contrary, it continuously changes and is variable. The different regions and neural networks are very dynamic.

A study by de Pasquale and colleagues (2012), using magnetoencephalography (MEG) to measure temporal change, showed that there is continuous change in the functional connectivity between different regions and networks of the brain. Interestingly, the midline regions—the ones that are strongly implicated in self-related processing—showed the greatest change and the most dynamics in connecting to other regions. That finding makes sense if we think of the person standing in the middle of a crowd, rather than on the periphery: That person can communicate the best and most easily with the others around him or her from that central position. Their position in the middle of the brain likewise predisposes the midline regions to communicate the most, that is, to connect to more regions and networks in the brain than other, noncentrally located regions.

Are the midline regions the seat of continuity over time and personal identity? The high degree of continuous change and variability in the midline regions, as well as activity and connectivity, speak against that. Rather than showing continuity over time, the midline regions can be characterized by discontinuity over time, change rather than identity. There is, though, some continuity in the midline regions: the *continuity of change*. There is continuous change and variability in activity levels and connectivity to other regions. And that change and variability seem to predispose the midline regions to be specifically implicated in processing self-relatedness or personal relevance, as we saw in Chapter 3. Hence our sense of self and our continuous experience of one and the same self over time seem to be mediated in yet unclear ways by the high degree of change and variability in the midline regions.

Is the continuity of person and self over time mediated by the discontinuity of the brain's resting-state activity? That sounds rather paradoxical. How can a person's continuity over time evolve from the brain's discontinuity over time? The philosopher focusing on logical coherence and afraid of logical inconsistencies and paradoxes would refrain from conceiving the midline region in particular and the brain in general as the seat of continuity over time and personal identity. The "I am my brain" statement therefore needs to be replaced by "I am not my brain."

Does the Brain's Discontinuity over Time Underlie the Person's Continuity?

How can we escape the paradox of discontinuity mediating continuity and identity? One way is to renounce identity and declare it to be irrelevant. Identity is neither here nor there, says the British philosopher Derek Parfit. Instead of assuming an "additional fact," Parfit rejects the notion of personal identity altogether and replaces it with the concept of survival. According to Parfit (1971, 1984), "what matters" is not "personal identity" but "survival" of the person. Unlike identity, survival implies neither a one-to-one nor an all-or-nothing relationship to the person. For example, in the case of the split between the two hemispheres of the brain, psychological continuity may be preserved so that the person "survives." Even though the person has two brains in such a case (i.e., the two hemispheres function separately), he or she nevertheless preserves a sense of psychological continuity, and that is all that matters (whereas identity does not matter).

However, the person cannot be considered as identical in the numerical sense, i.e., in terms of one person corresponding to (i.e., being identical with) another person, entailing a one-to-one relationship. Instead, in this case there is one person but two brains/hemispheres, amounting to a one-to-two and more-or-less relationship. "What matters" for the person in this case is therefore not numerical identity, and thus personal identity, but mere survival. Unlike the case of personal identity, the assumption of an additional fact is no longer necessary in survival. Instead, *survival* can be defined by the "Relation R," which Parfit characterizes as "psychological connectedness" and "psychological continuity" (1984, p. 206). Parfit's *psychological connectedness* points to direct psychological connections—for example, those between memories, as described by John Locke. In contrast, *psychological continuity* is defined by "overlapping chains of direct connectedness." Even if there are no direct connections—that is, if there is no psychological connectedness, as for example, in the case of amnesia— psychological continuity can nevertheless be maintained. Psychological continuity is therefore what matters for the survival of the person. As long as the right kind of psychological continuity is maintained in a person through time, this person survives, according to Parfit.

Parfit also challenges Nagel's (1974) assumption of identity as a nonconventional term. If the term *identity* were replaced by the term *survival*, the question of characterization of the latter has to be raised. Persons can survive without reference to something else, so the term *survival* can neither be characterized by an "empty position" nor an "additional fact," as suggested by Nagel. Parfit (1984) illustrates his point with an analogous example of nations. Although *nations* neither refer to a separate existing entity nor to other objects, properties, entities (e.g., governments, territory), they nevertheless survive. Analogous to nations, the term *survival* refers exclusively to itself. In contrast to Nagel, Parfit contends that the assumption of an "additional fact" is therefore no longer necessary (1984, pp. 471–472). Since there is no such "empty position," the brain is no longer needed for mere survival because survival is based on psychological continuity—which may (or may not) be caused by a brain, as Parfit says. But can we survive as persons without a brain?

Surviving without a brain sounds rather counterintuitive. Without brains, we do not survive. These days the death of the brain is equated with the death of the person. More specifically, if there is no electrical activity in the brain, as measured by electroencephalography (EEG), the brain is considered to be dead. Specifically, there is neither any *trace* of activity nor any *change* in activity anymore. The dead brain does finally fulfill the criterion of continuity over time: Nothing changes and everything remains the same with 100% continuity. The dead brain is identical with itself. The price for such continuity over time with identity is high, though; the brain is dead and does not function anymore. And even worse, the respectively associated person is also dead; there is no self or person anymore. The self has ceased to exist and is therefore discontinuous rather than continuous.

We are here confronted with another paradoxical situation, though in a reversed sense. In the case of the living brain, the discontinuity of its functioning is accompanied by the continuity of self and person. The brain's discontinuity over time leads to the person's continuity over time. The situation is reversed in the case of the dead brain. Here the brain is finally continuous over time, yet that does not entail continuity over time of the person and the self but the opposite: the discontinuity of self and person with their subsequent death.

How can we resolve this paradox? As a matter of fact, the brain and its resting-state activity can be characterized by discontinuity over time. That fact, in turn, seems to be highly relevant for establishing continuity over time of self and identity. Why? We have seen in schizophrenia that the continuity of the midline regions over time—that is, their change and variability—is abnormally altered, which in turn leads to discontinuity over time of self and person—that is, to identity change. Hence the brain's discontinuity over time must be related, in as yet unclear ways, to the continuity of self and identity over time. How is that possible? For a possible answer, we need to go deeper into the brain itself and investigate how its resting-state activity constructs time in a way that is related to the continuity of self and person over time.

Time and Self-Continuity

Am I my brain or not? Who is right: Nagel or Parfit? Is the brain the "additional fact" Nagel searches for, or is it irrelevant, as Parfit claims? How can we decide which of the two suggestions holds more veracity? One may apply purely conceptual and logical criteria and argue that the true suggestion would be logically and conceptually more consistent than the other. This is the way philosophers think. There has therefore been much debate over which of the criteria, brain or no brain, is logically more consistent with the notion of personal identity. The decision as to whether or not we are our brains is then a purely logical one.

Pure logic alone, however, is not what we really want. What we want are criteria that are not only logically consistent, as the philosopher strives for, but that also apply to the real world in which we live. For an answer that is both logical and reality-based, we need to venture from the purely logical territory of philosophy into the empirical territory of science, specifically neuroscience, and examine how neuroscience findings are related to the philosophical concepts. This is the very purpose of neurophilosophy.

In order to link the concept of personal identity to empirical findings in neuroscience, we first need to operationalize it. That is, we need to make the concept of personal identity empirically accessible. How can we operationalize the concept of personal identity? One way is to view personal identity in temporal terms and to operationalize or quantify the amount of time related to the continuity of the self—that is, its personal identity. Further considering the temporal element, a recent set of behavioral and imaging studies by the American scientist Ersner-Hershfield and his colleagues (Ersner-Hershfield, Wimmer, & Knutson, 2009) investigated the relationship between self-continuity and reward. They converted the philosophical concept of diachronic identity into a neuroscientific one. Recall that *diachronic identity* refers to the sense of continuity of a person or self over time, which may best be described by the term *self-continuity*. How can we now know whether the self is continuous or discontinuous across time? One empirical criterion for that is whether one perceives the self in the same way in the present and the future, and whether one acts in the same way now and later. Hence, similarity of perception and action between now and later, between present and future, can serve as empirical criterion to operationalize self-continuity.

This operationalization of the concept allows for testing across time in the context of reward. For instance, the experimenter could couple the presentation of a certain task with a reward, such as receiving some money, if the participant makes the correct decision. The experimenter could delay the delivery of the reward into the future, with different time intervals between the task and the reward delivery. This research condition is called *temporal discounting* (TD) because the longer the reward is delayed, the less the participants are usually interested in obtaining the reward, and consequently attribute less value to the stimulus.

Ersner-Hershfield, Wimmer, et al. (2009) coupled the perception of the self with such temporal discounting. By relating and correlating both measures, self-continuity and TD, they observed a negative correlation: the more increased the attenuation in TD (i.e., the further into the future the reward), the higher the degree to which self-continuity was perceived. This finding provides clear empirical evidence in favor of the relationship between self-continuity and temporal extension of the self into the future. In short, time and self-continuity seem to be intimately related, with both dependent on each other.

What do these results tell us about the relationship between continuity and time? The degree of continuity of the self and hence its identity is a matter of time. Longer time intervals lead to a decrease in the continuity of the self over time. Time constructs continuity in relation to discontinuity: Continuity over time stands in reciprocal balance to discontinuity such that increases in the latter entail decreases in the former (and vice versa). The longer the time intervals, the more that very same balance tilts toward discontinuity. I will experience my self as the same person but also as rather different when I am 20 years older. On the very next day, however, my experience of continuity is much higher and my experience of discontinuity rather low when compared to 20 years from now. There is a reciprocal balance along a continuum between continuity and discontinuity of self and person.

The continuum between continuity and discontinuity is a function of time. Time determines the balance between continuity and discontinuity. Once we get to the extremes of the two ends of the continuum between continuity and discontinuity, we are either dead or schizophrenic. In the case of 100% continuity of the brain, the brain is dead entailing the death of the person. In the opposite case of 100% discontinuity, the brain is disconnected from the world, transforming into discontinuity with identity change and the experience of a different self, as in schizophrenia.

Time Transforms Neuronal Discontinuity of the Brain into the Psychological Continuity of the Self

Is the relationship between self-continuity and time mediated and established by the brain? If so, one could argue that the brain, by mediating the link between self-continuity and time, is central for personal identity. Ersner-Hersfield and colleagues went beyond pure behavioral observations (Ersner-Hersfield, Garton et al. 2009) and studied the relationship between self-continuity and TD, using fMRI technology to reveal its neuronal mechanisms (Ersner-Hersfield, Wimmer et al., 2009). The researchers presented words that concerned each participant in the study. Most importantly, these words described participants' selves in the present and the future, thus implicating a sense of self across time, including its projection into the future.

Which area in the brain allows for the interaction between self-continuity and TD? The researchers observed that the perigenual anterior cingulate cortex (PACC) was a key area in mediating the interaction between self-continuity and TD. Hence, the PACC may be central in positioning the self in the stream of temporal continuity—from past to present to future—and, at the same time, linking it to value and reward. Most interestingly, we will see that the very same region, the PACC, is central in mediating self-relatedness as a core component of self, including its close relationship to the resting state of the brain.

What does this research tell us about personal identity and the brain? Personal identity is about linking self and time, thereby providing the kind of temporal self-continuity that defines our identity as persons. If that very same linkage is mediated and made possible by the brain, then the brain must be considered central for our personal identity. The brain and its neural mechanisms underlying the link between self and time may thus indeed be the "additional fact" for which Nagel was searching. Like the chemical formula underlying gold, the brain and its not yet fully understood neuronal mechanisms linking self and time may underlie what philosophers describe as personal identity.

Let's consider the known empirical side of things in more

detail. The midline regions show a high degree of variability and change and can thus be described as characterized by *neuronal discontinuity*. That neuronal discontinuity seems to be central in constructing psychological continuity of the self and hence what philosophers describe as personal identity. Neuronal discontinuity is essential for psychological continuity. This interconnection can be supported by the reverse case for which schizophrenia is a paradigmatic example. Disruption of the brain's neuronal discontinuity leads to disruption of the person's psychological continuity; in other words, neuronal continuity leads to psychological discontinuity, as we observed in Andrew, for instance.

We have to be careful, though. We saw that psychological continuity is not 100% but that it rather reflects a balance between continuity and discontinuity, which by itself is a function of time. If we now assume that the neuronal discontinuity of the brain mediates psychological continuity, we may want to investigate how the brain itself constructs time. That information, in turn, would establish a threefold relationship between brain, time, and continuity: Time as constructed on the basis of the brain's neuronal discontinuity will mediate the transformation of the neural messages of the brain into psychological continuity. Before we venture into the brain's construction of time, however, I need to defend another objection raised by the philosopher.

Schizophrenia versus Fetal Brain Tissue Transplantation

But wait, things are not so simple. The correlation between self-continuity and TD is just that: a correlation. It tells us nothing about whether the brain really causes the linkage between self-continuity and time, and hence personal identity. For that we need to investigate whether changes in the brain *cause* changes in self-continuity, and therefore in personal identity.

Patients with schizophrenia provide one useful area of investigation in this matter. As we saw in the previous chapter, patients with schizophrenia often experience their own self to be a different self, taking on the identities of famous people. In my life as a psychiatrist, I have encountered many such patients who claimed to be Jesus. One such patient grew a beard and wore a long, white shirt (or cape?). After asking him several times whether I could interview him, the patient, after giving no response for a long time, finally got up and said: "How could you dare speak to me like that? I am Jesus and I do not need to be interviewed."

Are there changes in the brains of patients with schizophrenia who exhibit such identity disturbances? As we saw, there are indeed major changes in their brain functioning, including in the PACC, the region that apparently links self and time. Schizophrenia therefore provides further evidence in favor of the intimate link between brain and personal identity.

Another test case may be patients who undergo deep brain stimulation (wherein an electrode is inserted into the brain) or even fetal brain tissue transplantation (fetal tissue is transplanted into the brain). Electrodes or fetal cells are inserted into subcortical regions in the brains of patients with Parkinson's disease, who suffer from motor disabilities, leaving them unable to walk (akinesia) as well as experiencing rigidity and tremors. In order to investigate the relationship between brain functioning and personal identity, I interviewed these patients with Parkinson's about their experiences of their own senses self and self-continuity—their personal identities (Northoff, 2001, 2004). Neither the disease itself nor the implant therapy was related subjectively (i.e., in the patients' personal experiences) or objectively (by the spouses) to any changes in their personal identities. Neither electrode stimulation nor fetal tissue was experienced as changing the identity; the fetal cells were regarded as a "natural and physiological substitute" for the dopamine deficiency in the brain. The electrode was considered a "technical device which makes the brain function in the correct way." One patient who spoke of "my electrode" also thought that the function of the electrode might be influenced by psychological factors, and that she "could influence the electrode emotionally and mentally." Another patient asked whether he would speak Swedish after the implantation (the surgery was performed in Sweden with fetal cells derived from Swedish fetuses).

What do these data tell us about the link between brain and personal identity? Even with electrodes or fetal cells implanted into the brain, patients do not experience a change in their personal identities. Is the brain thus not really necessary for personal identity? If so, Nagel would be wrong and Parfit would be right. The brain may not be essential for personal identity, which remains and can persist even when electrodes or fetal cells are inserted into the brain.

The neurophilosophical advocate of the brain as central to personal identity may argue, though, that it's not that simple. The example of schizophrenia demonstrates that changes in the brain *can* lead to changes in personal identity, as mediated by linking time and self in PACC. In contrast, insertion of electrodes or fetal tissue in subcortical regions does not impact personal identity. Maybe we need to investigate the PACC and see how the insertion of electrodes or fetal tissue into this region affects personal identity. For example, the neuroscientist Helen Mayberg (Mayberg et al. 2005) pioneered the use of deep brain stimulation in treating severe depression, by inserting an electrode into a region closely related to the PACC.

Key to this issue is to ask: What is the difference between schizophrenia and fetal brain tissue transplantation? Why does the one affect personal identity and its continuity, whereas the other one does not? Intuitively one would expect rather the reverse. In the case of fetal brain tissue transplantation, foreign material with genes from one (potential) person is transplanted into the brain of another person. If cells and brains are the seat of personal identity, one would expect the identity of the person who receives the fetal tissue to be changed. That, though, was not the case. Why?

In contrast, patients with schizophrenia *do* experience and exhibit changes in their personal identity. Why? Despite the fact that no foreign material is transplanted into their brains, they nevertheless experience discontinuity in their sense of self with subsequent identity change. How is that possible? We currently do not know. I postulate that time is central here. The resting-state activity of the brain may no longer properly construct time and its continuum between continuity and discontinuity in schizophrenia. That deficit, in turn, shifts the balance between continuity and discontinuity toward the one extreme, the pole of discontinuity; this translates into psychological discontinuity with subsequent loss of self and identity change.

Construction of Time by the Brain

How does the brain construct time? Various studies by, for instance, the Belgian researcher Antoine D'Argembeau and colleagues have demonstrated that the midline regions are central in constructing our sense of time (D'Argembeau et al., 2005; D'Argembeau, Feyers, et al., 2008; D'Argembeau et al., 2010a, 2010b; D'Argembeau, Xue, Lu, Van der Linden, & Bechara, 2008). He asked participants to imagine personally and nonpersonally relevant events in the future and the past. In both cases, future and past events, he observed strong activity changes especially in the cortical midline structures such as the ventro- and dorsomedial prefrontal cortex, the perigenual anterior cingulate cortex, and the posterior cingulate cortex.

What do these findings tell us about the construction of time? They suggest that the midline regions and their high degree of change and variability—their neuronal discontinuity—are central for constructing time. This implication has led another researcher, Dan Lloyd (2009), to the assumption that the midline regions can be conceived of as a "dynamic temporal network." How, though, can the continuously changing activity in these regions construct time, with its extensions into past and future? The midline regions and their changes show a broad spectrum of frequency ranges in their variability. The different frequency ranges operate on different time scales with either longer time scales in extremely slow frequency ranges from 0.001 Hz to 0.1 Hz, as measured in fMRI, or shorter time scales with frequency ranges from 1 to 180 Hz, as measured by EEG and MEG.

What do these different time scales in the resting-state

activity changes of the brain tell us about the construction of time? First and foremost they indicate that the resting-state activity includes different time scales. How are the different frequency ranges and their respective time scales related to each other? If they remain unrelated—that is, they do not interact with each other—and operate in parallel, one may speak of *temporal parallelism*. In that case there is only neuronal discontinuity but no neuronal continuity at all.

In contrast, if the different frequency ranges and their respective time scales are related to each other—that is, they are linked and integrated with each other—it could be measured in what is described as cross-frequency coupling. *Cross-frequency coupling* describes how the change in one frequency range is related time-wise to the change in another frequency range. For instance, the descending cycle in the one frequency range always occurs when the cycle ascends in the other frequency range. Cross-frequency coupling establishes a linkage between different frequency ranges and their time scales: The shorter time scale of change and its high degree of neuronal discontinuity is related to, even embedded within, the longer time scale and its lower degree of neuronal discontinuity (and higher degree of neuronal continuity). That, in turn, establishes a certain temporal structure with a balance between neuronal discontinuity and continuity.

How does the balance in the brain between neuronal discontinuity and continuity translate into psychological continuity? We currently do not know. What we *do* know is that the brain's resting-state activity in schizophrenia seems to show abnormally high degrees of neuronal discontinuity: The changes in the different frequency ranges are no longer coupled with each other, showing decreased cross-frequency coupling. The complex temporal structure of the healthy resting state is here replaced by a simpler temporal parallelism (for a more detailed explanation of this process, see Northoff, 2014c, 2015b).

Does the temporal parallelism in the resting-state activity of the brain account for the loss of psychological continuity and the subsequent identity changes in schizophrenia? We currently do not know. Given the central role of world–brain disruption in schizophrenia (see previous chapter), one may assume that the brain's construction of time is somehow decoupled from the world's construction of time. The continuous activity changes in the different frequency ranges and their different time scales are apparently decoupled from their corresponding "siblings" in the world that exhibit analogous frequency ranges and time scales. The world–brain relation may thus be disrupted in its temporal basis in schizophrenia.

Temporal Continuity Between Brain-Based Time and World-Based Time

These considerations lead us to an even deeper and rather philosophical issue: the relationship between time in the brain (i.e., brain-based time) and time in the world (world-based time). We have only a vague idea how the brain and its resting-state activity construct time (see Northoff, 2014c, 2015c). As indicated above, variability in the different frequency ranges and their respective time scales may be central. Even less known (if anything at all) is how the construction of time by the resting state, the brain-based time, is coupled with the time in the world, the world-based time. The healthy brain seems to construct its time in accordance with the time in the world by coupling and linking to it. Brain-based time is somehow in tune with world-based time. In short, brain-based time is (more or less) world-based time.

This intimate relationship between world- and brain-based time seems to be disrupted in schizophrenia. Here brain-based time is decoupled from world-based time: The patient with schizophrenia is decoupled from the time in his or her environment. The world–brain relation is temporally fragmented and disrupted.

How can we support such a claim of the temporal disruption in the world–brain relation? We can ask patients with schizophrenia how they themselves experience time in relation to events in the environment. Listen to this example of a patient's description in Fuchs's (2007) article: "When I move quickly, it is a strain on me. Things go too quickly for my mind. They get blurred and it is like being blind. It's as if you were seeing a picture one moment and another picture the next" (p.233). This patient is describing that his mental contents—for example, the different pictures—are no longer linked together temporally. There are no temporal transitions between the different discrete points in time and space associated with the different mental contents (e.g., pictures). Instead of temporal transitions, there are temporal gaps, which lead to temporal delays in linking the different mental contents and putting them together. Metaphorically speaking, the pictures are, as it were, experienced as pearls without an underlying chain. Since the underlying chain—the spatial–temporal continuity of the resting state—seems to be disrupted within itself, the pearls—the different mental contents—can no longer be put together, ordered, and structured in consciousness.

Consider this description by another patient:

"Each scene jumps over into the next, there is no coherence. Time is running strangely. It falls apart and no longer progresses. There arise only innumerable separate now, now, now—quite crazy and without rules or order. It is the same with myself. From moment to moment, various 'selves' arise and disappear entirely at random. There is no connection between my present ego and the one before" (Fuchs, 2013, p. 84).

This passage effectively describes the temporal gaps between the different mental contents, which can no longer be linked together temporally. The contents, the lived experiences, are merely unrelated slices of time. I assume that the missing temporal continuity is related to the lack of temporal continuity in resting-state activity of this person's brain, with decreased cross-frequency coupling. The absent temporal structure in resting-state activity makes it impossible to temporally integrate the various stimuli and their respective mental contents and thus to provide temporal linkage or a sense of continuity. That, in turn, leads to temporal gaps and temporal fragmentation during the experience of the various mental contents, which are then only experienced at different "now moments," we might say, without any temporal linkage. This description is well reflected in the following quote from a patient with schizophrenia: "Time splits up and doesn't run forward anymore. There arise uncountable disparate now, now, all crazy and without rule or order" (Martin, Giersch, Huron, & van Wassenhove, 2013, p. 361).

Coda: Existence, Time, and the Brain

What do these examples tell us about how time is perceived in the world and in the human brain? Healthy brains are able to construct some degree of temporal continuity between brain- and world-based time; brain-based time can align itself with world-based time. This alignment establishes temporal continuity between the individual and the surrounding world. In contrast, such alignment between brain- and world-based time seems to be disrupted in individuals with schizophrenia. As the preceding quotations indicate, these patients feel alienated within their subjective experience of time and detached from the ongoing time in the world.

The loss of the continuity of their sense of self over time culminates in eventual identity change that has deep metaphysical—or better, *existential*—implications. The brain and its resting state apparently connect us, in some as yet unclear ways, to the time of the world. The resulting temporal continuity between world- and brain-based time appears to be central for our existence: It allows us to locate our existence within the world and to experience the self as identical over time and as part of the world. Our existence within this world is brain-based due to the fact that the resting-state activity of the brain constructs temporal continuity between its own brain-based time and that of the world.

To be even more precise: Our existence is as much brain-based as it is time-based. It is the construction of brain-based time and its alignment to and temporal continuity with world-based time that makes our existence brain-based. This leads us back to the German philosopher Martin Heidegger, who argued at the beginning of the 20th century that our existence is based on time, that we are time, and,

Temporal frequency spectrum of the world

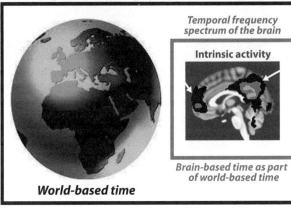

Temporal frequency spectrum of the brain

Intrinsic activity

Brain-based time as part of world-based time

World-based time

Figure 7.1 _____

even more importantly, we are *in* time—"Being is in time," as he said.

We can now see why and how such being or existence in time is possible. It is possible on the basis of the resting-state activity of the brain. Most importantly, this resting state allows us to continuously construct time, brain-based time, in close alignment with the world and its time, world-based time. We experience ourselves as part of the world and its time. The alignment of the brain and its brain-based time to the world and its time, world-based time, makes such "being in time" possible. Thanks to the brain, we are in the time of the world and can experience continuity over time in ourselves and in our personal identities. And thanks to such being in the time of the world, we exist within that very same world. Beyond that—the time of the world and our existence within its time—there is nothing at all, neither time nor existence.

REFERENCES

Alcaro, A., Panksepp, J., Witczak, J., Hayes, D. J., & Northoff, G. (2010). Is subcortical–cortical midline activity in depression mediated by glutamate and GABA?: A cross-species translational approach. *Neuroscience & Biobehavioral Reviews, 34*(4), 592–605. doi: 10.1016/j.neubiorev.2009.11.023.

Baars, B. J. (2005). Global workspace theory of consciousness: Toward a cognitive neuroscience of human experience. *Progress in Brain Research, 150,* 45–53. doi: 10.1016/S0079-6123(05)50004-9

Berze, J. (1914). *[The primary insufficiency of mental activity].* Leipzig, Germany: Franz Deuticke.

Bleuler, E. (1911). *[Dementia praecox or the group of schizophrenias].* New York: International Universities Press.

Bleuler, E. (1916). *[Textbook of psychiatry].* Berln: Heidelberg; New York: Springer.

Chalmers, D. J. (1996). *The conscious mind: In search of a fundamental theory.* New York: Oxford University Press.

Christoff, K., Cosmelli, D., Legrand, D., & Thompson, E. (2011). Specifying the self for cognitive neuroscience. *Trends in Cognitive Sciences, 15*(3), 104–112. doi: 10.1016/j.tics.2011.01.001.

Churchland, P. S. (2002). Self-representation in nervous systems. *Science, 12296*(5566), 308–310.

Craig, A. D. (2002). How do you feel? Interoception: The sense of the physiological condition of the body. *Nature Reviews Neuroscience, 3*(8), 655–666. doi: 10.1038/nrn894

Craig, A. D. (2003). Interoception: The sense of the physiological condition of the body. *Current Opinion in Neurobiology, 13*(4), 500–505.

Craig, A. D. (2004). Human feelings: Why are some more aware than others? *Trends in Cognitive Sciences, 8*(6), 239–241. doi: 10.1016/j.tics.2004.04.004

Craig, A. D. (2009a). Emotional moments across time: A possible neural basis for time perception in the anterior insula. *Philosophical Transactions of the Royal Society of London B: Biological Sciences, 364*(1525), 1933–1942.

Craig, A. D. (2009b). How do you feel—now?: The anterior insula and human awareness. *Nature Reviews Neuroscience, 10*(1), 59-70

Craig, A. D. (2010a). Once an island, now the focus of attention. *Brain Structure and Function, 214*(5–6), 395–396.

Craig, A. D. (2010b). The sentient self. *Brain Structure and Function, 214*(5–6), 563–577.

Craig, A. D. (2010c). Why a soft touch can hurt. *Journal of Physiology, 588*(Pt. 1), 13.

Craig, A. D. (2011). Interoceptive cortex in the posterior insula: Comment on Garcia-Larrea et al. 2010 Brain 133, 2528. *Brain, 134*(Pt. 4), e166.

Critchley, H. D., Wiens, S., Rotshtein, P., Ohman, A., & Dolan, R. J. (2004). Neural systems supporting interoceptive awareness. *Nature Neuroscience, 7*(2), 189–195. doi: 10.1038/nn1176

D'Argembeau, A., Collette, F., Van der Linden, L. M., Laureys, S., Del Fiore, G., Degueldre, C., . . . Salmon, E. (2005). Self-referential reflective activity and its relationship with rest: A PET study. *NeuroImage, 25*(2), 616–624.

D'Argembeau, A., Feyers, D., Majerus, S., Collette, F., Van der Linden, M., Maquet, P., & Salmon, E. (2008a). Self-reflection across time: Cortical midline structures differentiate between present and past selves. *Social Cognitive and Affective Neuroscience, 3*(3), 244–252. doi: 10.1093/scan/nsn020

D'Argembeau, A., Stawarczyk, D., Majerus, S., Collette, F., Van der Linden, M., Feyers, D., . . . Salmon, E. (2010a). The neural basis of personal goal processing when envisioning future events. *Journal of Cognitive Neuroscience, 22*(8), 1701–1713. doi: 10.1162/jocn.2009.21314

D'Argembeau, A., Stawarczyk, D., Majerus, S., Collette, F., Van der Linden, M., & Salmon, E. (2010b). Modulation of medial prefrontal and inferior parietal cortices when thinking about past, present, and future selves. *Social Neuroscience, 5*(2), 187–200.

D'Argembeau, A., Xue, G., Lu, Z. L., Van der Linden, M., & Bechara, A. (2008b). Neural correlates of envisioning emotional events in the near and far future. *NeuroImage, 40*(1), 398–407. doi: 10.1016/j.neuroimage.2007.11.025

Damasio, A. (1999). *The feeling of what happens: Body and emotion in the making of consciousness.* New York, NY: Harcourt Brace.

Damasio, A. (2010). *Self comes to mind: Constructing the conscious mind*. New York, NY: Pantheon.

de Greck, M., Wang, G., Yang, X., Wang, X., Northoff, G., & Han, S. (2012). Neural substrates underlying intentional empathy. *Social Cognitive and Affective Neuroscience, 7*(2), 135–144.

Dehaene, S., & Changeux, J. P. (2011). Experimental and theoretical approaches to conscious processing. *Neuron, 70*(2), 200–227. doi: 10.1016/j.neuron.2011.03.018

Dehaene, S., Charles, L., King, J.-R., & Marti, S. (2014). Toward a computational theory of conscious processing. *Current Opinion in Neurobiology, 25*, 76–84.

de Pasquale, F., Della Penna, S., Snyder, A. Z., Marzetti, L., Pizzella, V., Romani, G. L., & Corbetta, M. (2012). A cortical core for dynamic integration of functional networks in the resting human brain. *Neuron, 74*(4), 753–764.

Descartes, R. (1996). *Meditations on first philosophy* (J. Cottingham, Trans.). Cambridge, UK: Cambridge University Press (Original work published 1641)

Descartes, R., Weissman, D., & Bluhm, W. T. (1996). *Discourse on the method: And, meditations on first philosophy*. New Haven, CT: Yale University Press.

de Sousa, R. (2007). Emotion. In P. Goldie (Ed.), *The Oxford handbook of philosophy of emotion* (pp. 237–263). Oxford, UK: Oxford University Press.

Duncan, N. W., Hayes, D. J., Wiebking, C., Brice, T., Pietruska, K., Chen, D., . . . Northoff, G. (in press). Negative childhood experiences alter a prefrontal-insular-motor cortical network in healthy adults: A multimodal rsfMRI-fMRI-MRS-dMRI study. *Human Brain Mapping.*

Edelman, G. M. (2003). Naturalizing consciousness: A theoretical framework. *Proceedings of the National Academy of Sciences U.S.A., 100*(9), 5520–5524. doi: 10.1073/pnas.0931349100

Edelman, G. M. (2005). *Wider than the sky: A revolutionary view of consciousness*. London: Penguin.

Ersner-Hershfield, H., Garton, M. T., Ballard, K., Samanez-Larkin, G. R., & Knutson, B. (2009). Don't stop thinking about tomorrow: Individual differences in future self-continuity account for saving. *Judgment and Decision Making, 4*(4), 280–286.

Ersner-Hershfield, H., Wimmer, G. E., & Knutson, B. (2009). Saving for the future self: Neural measures of future self-continuity predict temporal discounting. *Social Cognitive and Affective Neuroscience, 4*(1), 85–92. doi: 10.1093/scan/nsn042

Ford, J. M., Morris, S. E., Hoffman, R. E., Sommer, I., Waters, F., McCarthy-Jones, S., . . . Cuthbert, B. N. (2014). Studying hallucinations within the NIMH RDoC framework. *Schizophrenia Bulletin, 40*(Suppl. 4), S295–S304. doi: 10.1093/schbul/sbu011.

Freton, M., Lemogne, C., Delaveau, P., Guionnet, S., Wright, E., Wiernik, E., . . . Fossati, P. (2014). The dark side of self-focus: brain activity during self-focus in low and high brooders. *Social Cognitive Affective Neuroscience, 9*(11), 1808–1813. doi: 10.1093/scan/nst178.

Fuchs, T. (2007). The temporal structure of intentionality and its disturbance in schizophrenia. *Psychopathology, 40*(4), 229–235.

Fuchs, T. (2013). Temporality and psychopathology. *Phenomenology and the Cognitive Sciences, 12*(1), 75–104.

Gallagher, S. (2005). *How the body shapes the mind.* Cambridge, UK: Cambridge University Press.

Golomb, J. D., McDavitt, J. R., Ruf, B. M., Chen, J. I., Saricicek, A., Maloney, K. H., . . . Bhagwagar, Z. (2009). Enhanced visual motion perception in major depressive disorder. *Journal of Neuroscience, 29*(28), 9072–9077. doi: 10.1523/JNEUROSCI.1003-09.2009.

Grimm, S., Ernst, J., Boesiger, P., Schuepbach, D., Boeker, H., & Northoff, G. (2011). Reduced negative BOLD responses in the default-mode network and increased self-focus in depression. *World Journal of Biological Psychiatry, 12*(8), 627–637. doi: 10.3109/15622975.2010.545145.

Heidegger, M. (2010). *Being and time* (J. Stambaugh, Trans., revised by D. J. Schmidt). Albany, NY: State University of New York Press. (Original work published 1927)

Hippocrates. (2006). *On the sacred disease.* Internet Classics Archive: University of Adelaide Library, archived from the original on September 26, 2007, retrieved December 17, 2006, from http://etext.library.adelaide.edu.au/mirror/classics.mit.edu/Hippocrates/sacred.html

Hoffman, R. E. (2007). A social deafferentation hypothesis for induction of active schizophrenia. *Schizophrenia Bulletin, 33*(5), 1066–1070.

Holt, D. J., Cassidy, B. S., Andrews-Hanna, J. R., Lee, S. M., Coombs, G., Goff, D. C., . . . Moran, J. M. (2011). An anterior-to-posterior shift in midline cortical activity in schizophrenia during self-reflection. *Biological Psychiatry, 69*(5), 415–423.

Hoptman, M. J., Zuo, X. N., Butler, P. D., Javitt, D. C., D'Angelo, D., Mauro, C. J., & Milham, M. P. (2010). Amplitude of low-frequency oscillations in schizophrenia: A resting state fMRI study. *Schizophrenia Research, 117*(1), 13–20.

Huang, Z., Dai, R., Wu, X., Yang, Z., Liu, D., Hu, J., . . . Northoff, G. (2014).

The self and its resting state in consciousness: An investigation of the vegetative state. *Human Brain Mapping, 35*(5), 1997–2008. doi: 10.1002/hbm.22308

Huang, Z., Wang, Z., Zhang, J., Dai, R., Wu, J., Li, Y., . . . Northoff, G. (2014). Altered temporal variance and neural synchronization of spontaneous brain activity in anesthesia. *Human Brain Mapping, 35*(11), 5341–5716. doi: 10.1002/hbm.22556

Huang, Z., Zhang, J., Wu, X., & Northoff, G. (2014). *Altered resting state variability in anesthesia.* Neuroimage, in press

Hume, D. (1777). *Enquiry concerning human understanding.* London: Milar. (Original work published 1748) Available online at http://www.davidhume.org/texts/ehu.html

Husserl, E. (1982). Ideas pertaining to a pure phenomenology and to a phenomenological philosophy (E. Kersten, Trans.). The Hague, Holland: Martinus Nijhoff Publisher. (Original work published 1913)

Ingram, R. E. (1990). Self-focused attention in clinical disorders: Review and a conceptual model. *Psychological Bulletin, 107*(2), 156–176.

James, W. (1890). *Principles of psychology* (2 Vols.). London: Dover.

Jaspers, K. (1997). *General psychopathology.* Chicago: University of Chicago Press. (Original work published 1964)

Javitt, D. C., & Freedman, R. (2015). Sensory processing dysfunction in the personal experience and neuronal machinery of schizophrenia. *American Journal of Psychiatry, 172*(1), 17–31. doi: 10.1176/appi.ajp.2014.13121691

Jones, W. H. S. (1868). *Hippocrates: Collected Works I.* Cambridge, MA: Harvard University Press. Retrieved September 28, 2006, from http://daedalus.umkc.edu/hippocrates/HippocratesLoebl/page.ix.php

Klein, S. B. (2012). Self, memory, and the self-reference effect: An examination of conceptual and methodological issues. *Personality and Social Psychology Review, 16*(3), 283–300. doi: 10.1177/1088868311434214

Klein, S. B., & Gangi, C. E. (2010). The multiplicity of self: Neuropsychological evidence and its implications for the self as a construct in psychological research. *Annals of the New York Academy of Sciences, 1191*, 1–15. doi: 10.1111/j.1749-6632.2010.05441.x

Kraeplin, E. (1913). *[A textbook of psychiatry for students and doctors].* Leipzig, Germany: Barth.

Lashley, K. S. (1949). Persistent problems in the evolution of mind. *Quarterly Review of Biology, 24*(1), 28–42.

LeDoux, J. E. (2003). *Synaptic self: How our brains become who we are*. New York, NY: Penguin.

Lewis, D. A. (2014). Inhibitory neurons in human cortical circuits: Substrate for cognitive dysfunction in schizophrenia. *Current Opinion in Neurobiology, 26*, 22–26. doi: 10.1016/j.conb.2013.11.003.

Lipsman, N., Nakao, T., Kanayama, N., Krauss, J. K., Anderson, A., Giacobbe, P., . . . Northoff, G. (2014). Neural overlap between resting state and self-relevant activity in human subcallosal cingulate cortex: Single unit recording in an intracranial study. *Cortex, 60*, 139–144. doi: 10.1016/j.cortex.2014.09.008

Lloyd, D. M. (2009). The space between us: A neurophilosophical framework for the investigation of human interpersonal space. *Neuroscience & Biobehavioral Reviews, 33*(3), 297–304.

MacDougall, D. (1907). Hypothesis concerning soul substance together with experimental evidence of the existence of such substance. *Journal of the American Society of Psychical Research, 1*(5), 237–244.

Martin, B., Giersch, A., Huron, C., & van Wassenhove, V. (2013). Temporal event structure and timing in schizophrenia: Preserved binding in a longer "now." *Neuropsychologia, 51*(2), 358–371. doi: 10.1016/j.neuropsychologia.2012.07.002

Mayberg HS, Lozano AM, Voon V, McNeely HE, Seminowicz D, Hamani C, Schwalb JM, Kennedy SH. (2005) Deep brain stimulation for treatment-resistant depression. Neuron. 2005 Mar 3;45(5):651-60.

McGinn, C. (1991) The problem of consciousness. Blackwell Publisher, London

Medford, N., & Critchley, H. D. (2010). Conjoint activity of anterior insular and anterior cingulate cortex: Awareness and response. *Brain Structure and Function, 214*(5–6), 535–549. doi: 10.1007/s00429-010-0265-x

Merleau-Ponty, M. (1962). Phenomenology of perception (C. Smith, Trans.). London: Routledge. (Original work published 1945)

Metzinger, T. (2004). *Being no one: The self-model theory of subjectivity*: Cambridge, MA: MIT Press.

Monti, M., Vanhaudenhuyse, A., Coleman, M., Boly, M., Pickard, J., Tshibanda, L., . . . Laureys, S. (2010). Willful modulation of brain activity in disorders of consciousness. *New England Journal of Medicine, 362*(7), 579–589.

Nagel, T. (1974). What is it like to be a bat? *The Philosophical Review, 83*, 435–450.

Northoff, G. (2001).Personal identity and surgical interventions into the brain. Paderborn, Germany: Mentis Publisher.

Northoff, G. (2004). *Philosphy of the brain*. Amsterdam/New York: John Benjamins.

Northoff, G. (2007). Psychopathology and pathophysiology of the self in depression - neuropsychiatric hypothesis. *Journal of Affective Disorders*, *104*(1–3):1–14.

Northoff, G. (2012). From emotions to consciousness: A neuro-phenomenal and neuro-relational approach. *Frontiers in Psychology*, *3*, 303. doi: 10.3389/fpsyg.2012.00303

Northoff, G. (2013). Gene, brains, and environment–genetic neuroimaging of depression. *Current Opinion in Neurobiology*, *23*(1), 133–142.

Northoff, G. (2014a). Are auditory hallucinations related to the brain's resting state activity?: A "neurophenomenal resting state hypothesis." *Clinical Psychopharmacology and Neuroscience*, *12*(3), 189–195. doi: 10.9758/cpn.2014.12.3.189.

Northoff, G. (2014b). *Unlocking the brain: Vol. 1. Coding*. New York, NY: Oxford University Press.

Northoff, G. (2014c). *Unlocking the brain: Vol. II. Consciousness*. New York, NY: Oxford University Press.

Northoff, G. (2014d). Minding the brain: A guide to philosophy and neuroscience. Palgrave MacMillan,London, New York

Northoff, G. (2015a). Is schizophrenia a spatiotemporal disorder of the brain's resting state? *World Psychiatry, 14*(1), 34–35.

Northoff, G. (2015b). Resting state activity and the "stream of consciousness" in schizophrenia—neurophenomenal hypotheses. *Schizophr Bull, 41*(1), 280-290. doi: 10.1093/schbul/sbu116

Northoff G. (2015c) Slow cortical potentials and "inner time consciousness" - A neuro-phenomenal hypothesis about the "width of present."Int J Psychophysiol. 2015 Feb 9. pii: S0167-8760(15)00042-2. doi: 10.1016/j.ijpsycho.2015.02.012.

Northoff G. (2015d) Do cortical midline variability and low frequency fluctuations mediate William James' "Stream of Consciousness"? "Neurophenomenal Balance Hypothesis" of "Inner Time Consciousness".Conscious Cogn. :184-200. doi: 10.1016/j.concog.2014.09.004. Epub 2014 Oct 6.

Northoff G.(in press) Spatiotemporal psychopathology I: No rest for the brain's resting state activity in depression? Spatiotemporal psychopathology of depressive symptoms. J Affect Disord. 2015 May 14. pii: S0165-0327(15)00299-2. doi: 10.1016/j.jad.2015.05.007. [Epub ahead of print] Review.

Northoff G. (in press) Spatiotemporal Psychopathology II: How does a psychopathology of the brain's resting state look like? Spatiotemporal approach and the history of psychopathology. J Affect Disord. 2015 May 19. pii: S0165-0327(15)00300-6. doi: 10.1016/j.jad.2015.05.008. [Epub ahead of print] Review.

Northoff, G., Heinzel, A., de Greck, M., Bermpohl, F., Dobrowolny, H., & Panksepp, J. (2006). Self-referential processing in our brain: A meta-analysis of imaging studies on the self. *NeuroImage, 31*(1), 440–457.

Northoff, G., Qin, P., & Nakao, T. (2010). Rest–stimulus interaction in the brain: A review. *Trends in Neuroscience, 33*(6), 277–284.

Olson, E. T. (1997). *The human animal: Personal identity without psychology*. Oxford, UK: Oxford University Press.

Owen, A., Coleman, M., Boly, M., Davis, M., Laureys, S., & Pickard, J. (2006). Detecting awareness in the vegetative state. *Science, 313*(5792), 1402.

Panksepp, J. (1998a). *Affective neuroscience: The foundations of human and animal emotions*: New York, NY: Oxford University Press.

Panksepp, J. (1998b). The preconscious substrates of consciousness: Affective states and the evolutionary origins of the SELF. *Journal of Consciousness Studies, 5*, 566–582.

Panksepp, J. (2007a). Affective consciousness. In M. Velmans & S. Schneider (Eds.), *The Blackwell companion to consciousness* (pp. 114–129). New York: Wiley.

Panksepp, J. (2007b). The neuroevolutionary and neuroaffective psychobiology of the prosocial brain. *The Oxford handbook of evolutionary psychology* (pp. 145–162). Oxford, UK: Oxford University Press.

Panksepp, J. (2011a). The basic emotional circuits of mammalian brains: Do animals have affective lives? *Neuroscience & Biobehavioral Reviews, 35*(9), 1791–1804.

Panksepp, J. (2011b). Cross-species affective neuroscience decoding of the primal affective experiences of humans and related animals. *PLoS One, 6*(9), e21236.

Parfit, D. (1971). Personal identity. *Philosophical Review, 80*, 3–27.

Parfit, D. (1984). *Reasons and persons*: Oxford, UK: Oxford University Press.

Parnas, J. (2003). Self and schizophrenia: A phenomenological perspective. In T. Kircher & A. David (Eds.), *The self in neuroscience and psychiatry* (pp. 217–241). Cambridge, UK: Cambridge University Press.

Parnas, J., Vianin, P., Saebye, D., Jansson, L., Volmer-Larsen, A., &

Bovet, P. (2001). Visual binding abilities in the initial and advanced stages of schizophrenia. *Acta Psychiatrica Scandinavica, 103*(3), 171–180.

Pomarol-Clotet, E., Salvador, R., Sarro, S., Gomar, J., Vila, F., Martinez, A., . . . McKenna, P. J. (2008). Failure to deactivate in the prefrontal cortex in schizophrenia: Fysfunction of the default mode network? *Psychological Medicine, 38*(8), 1185–1193.

Qin, P., & Northoff, G. (2011). How is our self related to midline regions and the default-mode network? *NeuroImage, 57*(3), 1221–1233.

Raichle, M. E. (2009). A brief history of human brain mapping. *Trends in Neuroscience, 32*(2), 118–126.

Raichle, M. E. (2010). The brain's dark energy. *Scientific American, 302*(3), 44–49.

Raichle, M. E., MacLeod, A. M., Snyder, A. Z., Powers, W. J., Gusnard, D. A., & Shulman, G. L. (2001). A default mode of brain function. *Proceedings of the National Academy of Sciences U.S.A, 98*(2), 676–682.

Ratcliffe, M. (2008). *Feelings of being: Phenomenology, psychiatry and the sense of reality.* International Perspectives in Philosophy & Psychiatry. New York: Oxford University Press.

Rolls, E. T. (2000). The representation of umami taste in the taste cortex. *Journal of Nutrition, 130*(4S Suppl.), 960S–965S.

Rolls, E. T., Tovee, M. J., & Panzeri, S. (1999). The neurophysiology of backward visual masking: Information analysis. *Journal of Cognitive Neuroscience, 11*(3), 300–311.

Sadaghiani S, Hesselmann G, Friston KJ, Kleinschmidt A. (2010) The relation of ongoing brain activity, evoked neural responses, and cognition. Front Syst Neurosci. 2010 Jun 23;4:20. doi: 10.3389/fnsys.2010.00020. eCollection 2010.

Sanacora, G., Mason, G. F., & Krystal, J. H. (2000). Impairment of GABAergic transmission in depression: New insights from neuroimaging studies. *Critical Reviews in Neurobiology*, 14(1), 23–45.

Sass, L. A. (2003). Self-disturbance in schizophrenia: Hyperreflexivity and diminished self-affection. In T. Kircher & A. David (Eds.), *The self in neuroscience and psychiatry* (pp. 128-148). Cambridge, UK: Cambridge University Press.

Schachter, S., & Singer, J. (1962). Cognitive, social, and physiological determinants of emotional state. *Psychological Review, 69*(5), 379–399. doi: 10.1037/h0046234

Schilbach, L., Bzdok, D., Timmermans, B., Fox, P.T., Laird, A.R., Vogeley, K., & Eickhoff, S.B. (2012). Introspective minds: Using ALE meta-analyses to study commonalities in the neural correlates of emotional processing, social and unconstrained cognition. *PLoS One*, *7*(2), e30920. doi: 10.1371/journal.pone.0030920.

Schilbach, L., Eickhoff, S.B., Rotarska-Jagiela, A., Fink, G.R., & Vogeley, K. (2008). Minds at rest?: Social cognition as the default mode of cognizing and its putative relationship to the "default system" of the brain. *Conscious Cognition*, *17*(2), 457–67. doi: 10.1016/j.concog.2008.03.013.

Schneider, F, Bermpohl, F, Heinzel, A, Rotte, M, Walter, M, Tempelmann, C, . . . Northoff G. (2008). The resting brain and our self: Self-relatedness modulates resting state neural activity in cortical midline structures. Neuroscience, *157*(1), 120–131. doi: 10.1016/j.neuroscience.2008.08.014.

Schopenhauer, A. (1966a). *The world as will and idea* (Vol. 1). London: Dover. (Original work published 1818)

Schopenhauer, A. (1966b). *The world as will and idea* (Vol. 2). London: Dover. (Original work published 1819)

Searle, J. R. (2004). *Mind: A brief introduction* (Vol. 259). New York, NY: Oxford University Press.

Stanghellini, G., Ballerini, M., Presenza, S., Mancini, M., Raballo, A., Blasi, S., & Cutting, J. (2015). Psychopathology of lived time: Abnormal time experience in persons with schizophrenia. *Schizophrenia Bulletin* pii: sbv052.

Stanghellini G, Ballerini M, Presenza S, Mancini M, Raballo A, Blasi S, Cutting J. (2015) Psychopathology of Lived Time: Abnormal Time Experience in Persons With Schizophrenia. Schizophr Bull. 2015 May 4. pii: sbv052.

Stanghellini, G., & Rosfort, R. (2015). Disordered selves or persons with schizophrenia? *Current Opinion in Psychiatry*, *28*(3), 256–263. doi: 10.1097/YCO.0000000000000155.

Tononi, G. (2012). Integrated information theory of consciousness: An updated account. *Archives Italiennes de Biologie, 150*(2–3), 56–90.

Tononi, G., & Koch, C. (2015). Consciousness: Here, there and everywhere? *Philosophical Transactions of the Royal Society of London B: Biological Sciences, 370*(1668), 20140167.

Treynor, W., Gonzalez, R., & Nolen-Hoeksema, S. (2003). Rumination reconsidered: A psychometric analysis. *Cognitive Therapy and Research, 27*(3), 247–259.

Whitfield-Gabrieli, S., Thermenos, H. W., Milanovic, S., Tsuang, M. T., Faraone, S. V., McCarley, R. W., . . . LaViolette, P. (2009). Hyperactivity and hyperconnectivity of the default network in schizophrenia and in first-degree relatives of persons with schizophrenia. *Proceedings of the National Academy of Sciences, 106*(4), 1279–1284.

Wiebking, C., Bauer, A., de Greck, M., Duncan, N. W., Tempelmann, C., & Northoff, G. (2010). Abnormal body perception and neural activity in the insula in depression: An fMRI study of the depressed "material me." *World Journal of Biological Psychiatry, 11*(3), 538–549.

Wiebking, C., Duncan, N. W., Tiret, B., Hayes, D. J., Marjańska, M., Doyon, J., Bajbouj, M., & Northoff, G. (2014). GABA in the insula: A predictor of the neural response to interoceptive awareness. *NeuroImage, 86*, 10–18. doi: 10.1016/j.neuroimage.2013.04.042.

Zahavi, D. (2005). *Subjectivity and selfhood: Investigating the first-person perspective.* Cambridge, MA: MIT press.

INDEX

Note: Italicized page locators indicate figures.